THE
POOR OLD
LIBERAL
ARTS

BOOKS BY ROBERT I. GANNON

After Black Coffee
The Poor Old Liberal Arts
The Technique of the One-Act Play

THE
POOR OLD
LIBERAL
ARTS

Robert I. Gannon

FARRAR, STRAUS & CUDAHY

NEW YORK

CONTENTS

FOREWORD

Towards evening it is everyone's privilege to relax and think out loud without too much intellectual discipline. As the shadows begin to lengthen in the room, a man can stand his scholarly apparatus in the corner and use all the itchy references and footnotes as they should be used—to light the fire on the hearth.

So it was that having known the liberal arts for half a century and watched with sympathy their struggle to survive even in Jesuit universities and colleges, the author was thinking out loud when he gave the Ledesma Lecture on November 15, 1958, at Loyola University, Los Angeles. It was just a matter of a pleasant hour with a sympathetic audience, but printed afterwards in the alumni paper it came to the attention of the present publishers, who asked that it be expanded into a little book.

The autobiographical form is just an old evergreen on which to hang some tinsel and one or two angels.

My thanks go out to Fathers Thomas J. M. Burke, Donald R. Campion, Thurston N. Davis, Allan P. Farrell, Paul A. FitzGerald, Matthew J. Fitzsimons, Neil J. McCluskey and Edward L. Murphy, all of the Society, who were good enough to plough through the manuscript. They were not of one mind on every issue but made invaluable suggestions.

ROBERT I. GANNON, S.J.

The Feast of The Epiphany,
1961

THE
POOR OLD
LIBERAL
ARTS

I

In Another World

IT IS STILL CONSIDERED SOMETHING to have made one's studies in a foreign country. A graduate so fortunate can come home with a touch of an accent, a good deal of an air, and comparative immunity from investigation. He can always be mysteriously modest about his scholastic rank. But the really fortunate ones are those who have had a chance to make their studies not in a different country but in a different world.

The spacemen in grammar school might take that in one sense and the classicists who have soaked themselves in, let us say, the world of Pericles might take it in another, but here it is meant to refer to those whose lives span a period not only of transition but of transformation. St. Thomas More went to Oxford in one world and died in another. Lafayette was commissioned in one world, acclaimed in a second, denounced in a third, and buried in a fourth. In like manner it can be said of the old gaffers who finished college before 1914, they prepared for life in a world that no longer exists.

Many might regard this as a serious handicap because they think of human development in terms of nuclear power. What good is a horse-and-buggy education—liberal arts and all that—for one who has to live with the ghost of Hiroshima? If an age is materialistic and pragmatic, the only fit preparation for it is one that is materialistic and pragmatic. Education should be content to mirror contemporary society and not try to lead it anywhere.

Such a viewpoint, of course, overlooks a number of values, beginning with the general value of a point of reference. One may enjoy but cannot evaluate a work of art, or a pudding, or a ball game unless a few comparisons are brought into play. And so it is with the world of the 1960s. It can be taken for granted by a youngster who has never known any other and can even be relished now and then in a one-dimensional kind of way, but its abnormality cannot be fully recognized except by those who have known a normal year.

The year 1909 was a normal one, though it could look back on plenty of excitement. The parents of a certain Georgetown freshman who entered college that fall could remember the Civil War distinctly. One of his old teachers could remember Daniel Webster dining on boiled ham with the Fathers at Whitemarsh, and the freshman himself could recall standing on a cracker barrel with a little flag and waving at Admiral Dewey as he rode down Pennsylvania Avenue in triumph after the Battle of Manila. As a fourteen-year-old he had been in Paris walking in the gardens of the Tuileries with one of his elders who recognized an old lady seated on a bench, feeding the birds with bread crumbs. She was alone, dressed in black, very dignified, very sweet looking. It was the Empress Eugenie. That same year he met one of Garibaldi's veterans in Sorrento, still flaunting a red shirt, and an Englishman, not so old either, who had fought with Chinese Gordon at Khartoum. 1909 could certainly look back on plenty of excitement, but it was a normal year.

There was world peace, and a heavy quiet had settled in the White House since the storm center was in Africa shooting lions. The Chancellories of

Europe were nervous, but that was normal. The Balkans showed signs of restlessness, but that was normal too; Graustark and Ruritania were always at the boiling point. There were headlines during the spring, when Robert E. Peary reached the North Pole and in mid-Summer when Louis Bleriot flew the English Channel at a speed of nearly 60 miles an hour, but to a Freshman entering Georgetown on a warm afternoon in late September, the world around him seemed the most ordinary of all possible worlds. In fact three years later when as a Senior he had the right to sit on the steps of the Old North and appraise the universe through clouds of Fatimas and Melachrinos, he agreed with his contemporaries that they had lived too late. The last page of colorful history had been written. There would never be another war. There was only one struggle of which the young man was vaguely aware at the time, a struggle with newfangled ideas that were undermining what he had always considered the foundations of education.

Georgetown back in 1909 consisted of a small Prep School, a small College, 120 students in all; a small Medical School of undetermined classification (the term Class A was still unused), and a large Law School. In college there was only one degree, Bachelor of Arts, except for those strangers within the gates who could not make head or tail of Latin and Greek even with a trot. They received a Bachelor of Science as a kind of receipt for their tuition. The rich curriculum in the liberal arts was determined for the candidate by his elders except for one elective in Junior and one in Senior, and accepted without question or much enthusiasm. For it must be admitted at the outset that college students 50 years ago did not on the whole, work as hard as their successors have to work today. It was too easy to get into college and much too easy to stay there, a condition that made motivation too frequently uncertain. To one, a college course was just an experience that a young man had coming to him, like a summer at the shore. To another, it was a pre-professional requirement or the backdrop of an athletic program. To a third, it was a chance to get away from home where the family even then persisted in treating a Freshman as if he had been a high school boy the year before. So that as we see it today, the arts course in 1909 was still a great opportunity though too often a wasted one.

Here and there an intellectual appeared who relished his work for what it was. Such a phenomenon was promptly classified as a grind unless he happened to be the type of genius who could stroke the crew, stay out nights and still get honor cards. (There was a crew in 1909 and our indomitable Freshman, who weighed in at 96 pounds even after being tossed into the Potomac, was coxswain of the second boat!) In all justice to the era it must be confessed that if a young man in those unregenerate days had told the Prefect of Studies that he came to the University because he felt that a true college of liberal arts ranks with the family, the church, and the courts of law as one of the four great nerves of tradition, Georgetown would have declared a holiday. And if any parent at that time had been bold enough to say to his son, "My boy, I am sending you to college so that you may some day pass on to the next generation the spiritual and intellectual heritage of the Western World," he would even then have sounded like a voice from the grave, the confident voice of the buried 19th Century. Something had already happened to the liberal arts.

It is true that in 1909 Queen Victoria was more recent than Franklin Roosevelt is today, but many horizons were being pushed back. Unknown to us the nuclear age had already begun. (Einstein had published his formula on the relation of energy to matter.) Progressive Education had already reared its lovely head. (John Dewey was settled at Columbia, and giving tradition short shrift.) The United States Supreme Court was already de-emphasizing the natural law and the Constitution was getting nervous. (Oliver Wendell Holmes had taken over as Associate Justice.) Many other changes too were in the air and Jesuit colleges like their conservative neighbors were in an age of adjustment. They were also, if the truth must be known, in something of a fog.

More than half a century had passed since a quaint book appeared in Boston, written by a Yale Professor, and entitled *The Educational Systems of the Puritans and Jesuits Compared* (Ed. Porter, 1851). It was a good old cry of Protestant alarm that pointed out how much more effective the Jesuits were than the Puritans. A place called the College of the Holy Cross had opened in Worcester, Massachusetts, a dazzling, dangerous place where the spirit of severe and iron industry was equalled only by the severity of the discipline. With regard to the faculty, it had this to say: "The Jesuit comes from the best colleges of Europe, he has been a student since infancy under exact and skillful teachers; he has been familiar with prodigies of learning from the first; he has mastered the modern languages in a way that is to an American a marvel and a mystery." More important are the author's observations of our methods of instruction. "These," he says, "are rigorous and thorough. The student is drilled to such a control of what he learns that it will

[7]

be a possession for life. The teachers' methods have been tested for generations; his books are the works of the ablest men of his Order so that he is never distracted by experimenting with new devices." Finally he comments on our general conditions, pointing out that "ample and learned libraries are at their command, costly and substantial edifices are located in the choicest situations and the instruction is practically gratuitous." The rest is too good to omit. "Last of all, there is no ruinous competition, nor degrading jealousies between their several institutions and they are never multiplied to the impoverishment of their several faculties or the degradation of sound learning."

Granted that the picture was even then a very flattering one, highlighted by the fear of a Puritan author, there was ample foundation for at least some of the details.

The Jesuit libraries a hundred years ago, modest as they were, compared favorably with those around them. (I remember Nicholas Murray Butler saying one time that, when he was a boy, Columbia had fewer books on its shelves than a good high school would need today.) Their buildings were considered elegant in an era of great simplicity and most of their men had been trained in Europe because there was no place over here properly manned. What really mattered however was the fact that they were not at that time "distracted by experimenting with new devices," nor were they to be distracted for another forty years. Until almost the end of the 19th Century they knew where they were going and how to get there. They had a code already two hundred and fifty years old, commonly known as the *Ratio Studiorum.* This had been published in 1599 as the *Ratio atque Institutio Studiorum Societatis Jesu* or "The Jesuit Code of Liberal Education." It was the result of more than thirty-five years of experimentation with an earlier plan edited by Fr. James Ledesma, the first Dean or Praefectus Studiorum of the Roman College. The curriculum it outlined embraced three years of grammar, one of humanities or belles lettres, whose specific object was the appreciation of beauty; one of rhetoric which centered chiefly on the study of elo-quence and a final year of philosophy, pure science and mathematics.

In the United States the Jesuits began with four grammar grades leading to Belles Lettres and Rheto-ric, and added the year of Philosophy only in 1816, when they were preparing to give the first B.A.s at Georgetown. By 1839 Philosophy had become a pre-requisite to any degree in all American Jesuit colleges, but the second year of philosophy was introduced only at the turn of the century. Meanwhile the pressure of the four year college custom around them had led Georgetown in 1851 to promote one grammar grade into the higher echelon, so that they had three grammar grades, and a college course of Philosophy, Rhetoric, Belles Lettres and Prosody. This separation even on paper of the upper and lower classes did not help the humanistic synthesis of the *Ratio Studiorum*, but the damage was not apparent until the Colleges with their own administration moved away from the High Schools—a development that was only beginning in 1909.

The methods outlined in the 16th Century with much detail held the line longer, however, than the class divisions and gave the Jesuits down to the end of the 19th Century a sense of security and a mark of distinction. Like all the good things of life these methods were not entirely new. The school masters of the Renaissance in freeing themselves from the lecture routine of the Middle Ages all looked to Quintilian for inspiration, and Ignatius was no exception. But the old Roman's reliable pedagogy had been modified by the experience gained in hundreds of Jesuit classrooms for 50 years before appearing in the *Ratio Studiorum*. There the ancient principles of preparation, repetition, and emulation were still recognizable, but on being given fresh forms became known as Jesuit methods. These included first the "Prelection," which differed in the upper and lower classes. Although the earliest application of the Prelection was made to Latin and Greek, it was readily adaptable to the teaching of history, mathematics, pure science and modern languages. For the little fellows, the passage assigned for the next day was read aloud with much expression, word lists were compiled, and the difficult parsing explained. Their older brothers were warned about idiomatic expressions and given hints on style. Added to this was the study of what our ancestors called "Erudition." This covered a rather elaborate treatment of history, geography, art, ethnology and so forth, insofar as they might be needed for a full appreciation of the author. The real heart of the *Ratio* was "Composition," which stressed the all important art of expression. The daily themes, which in the upper classes were supposed to imitate the style of the author being studied at the moment, not only kept syntax fresh in mind but developed a healthy appreciation for literary effort. Only when a boy had poured a few drops of blood into creating a Sapphic and Adonic could he really give Horace his due, and who could ever taste the flavor of a periodic sentence in Cicero until he had thrown around a few *"esse videaturs"* himself?

Returning to class after due preparation, the student anticipated not only simple recitation but "Discussion," and this ran the gamut from formal disputation in the higher classes to contests and games in the lower. The disputations were modeled on the "circles" that had been familiar features in medieval universities. One student would defend some proposition that was made about the author, for example his superiority to another author who was known to the class, while two objectors plied him with difficulties. Others put questions *"ex corona"* that is to say, from the floor. Beginners on the other hand, ran what were known as *"concertationes."* These could take the form of football games with a gridiron drawn on the board and a suspended ball that was advanced through elaborate rules toward a goal, or war games with Greek phalanxes that moved inch by inch against Persian strongholds, or any other sort of fascinating beguilement. All this involved well-balanced teams with plenty of excitement and rewards that disguised the drudgery of drill work. Repetition was frequent and the amount of refreshing variety that could be introduced measured a teacher's skill. Anyone who was so lacking in invention that he had to descend to the level of a lecture in a lower grade was regarded even by the students as a failure. The matter was always taken with great thoroughness, a little at a time and carefully graded to produce a cumulative effect.

Outside of class "Academies" were prescribed, that is, groups of homogeneous students. Some of these were reading more extensively than the syllabus required (all of Homer's *Iliad* for example or all of Seneca's tragedies); some, less advanced, were building triremes and amphitheatres; others were writing or performing plays. Drama from the beginning was almost an individuating note of a Jesuit college. In Sommervogel's monumental work *Bibliothèque de la Compagnie de Jesus* the titles of plays which the Fathers and their students wrote and produced, especially in 17th Century France, cover several large pages of small type.

In all this the Jesuits always liked to feel that they were training liberal arts students to be intellectual leaders and, until the 19th century, kept them in their colleges for six years. The boy entered at about the age of twelve, and graduated with an A.B. at about eighteen. From the very beginning, underlying their idea of the liberal arts college were two presuppositions, both of which seemed obvious enough in 1860, both of which are vigorously challenged by our neighbors in 1960 with what seem to be disastrous results. First, it was always believed in their schools that all men have the same principal purpose in life and that that purpose is discoverable. It is no secret, except to the most "advanced," that man was made to praise, reverence and serve God and thereby save his soul. Second, it was always believed that all men have faculties which are capable of being trained, group them and name them as you like as long as they cover broadly the intellect and the will. So that even before the curriculum, method and discipline of a liberal education had been thought through, the early Jesuits were satisfied that learning was not an end in itself but a means whose end was to make men more human and more spiritual, better able to live freely and fully here, and attain the ultimate purpose of their existence.

They realized that general culture should precede specialization; that this general culture should not be appraised in terms of immediate utility, like courses in a trade school; that the first responsibility of a college of liberal arts should center not on facts or skills, but on attitudes; that its primary task should be the refining of taste, the sharpening of intellect, the strengthening of will, the ennobling of character. They felt too, as true children of the Renaissance, that in achieving these ends, Latin, Greek and Philosophy formed a constant that could be relied upon as at least *one* external approach to art, literature, sociology, history, politics and pure science. Their regard for the culture of Greece and Rome was once eloquently expressed by the late Father Jaime Castiello S.J., in *A Humane Psychology of Education.* He wrote: "This classical culture when carried out under Christian auspices does give a true, inward, almost experimental knowledge of that which is spiritual; something that cannot be reduced to time, space, weight or number; something which is essentially fluid, moving, plastic, rich and capable of holding in itself the whole of creation—a microcosmos: something which in its immense, opulent, interior life is yet immensely lonely, poor and ardently thirsty for God."

If this devotion of the early Jesuits to Latin and Greek was essentially modern in 1599 (and they were pioneers in systematizing the teaching of the classics), their unshaken loyalty to scholastic philosophy was considered at the dawn of the 17th century a little out of date. The glorious thirteenth century, the century of Albertus Magnus and Thomas Aquinas, meant olden times to them, as olden as theirs is to us today, but they stoutly maintained that the science of ultimate causes, that is philosophy, systematically pursued is essential to a balanced grasp of any other science, social or physical; that it is, besides, one of the principal coordinators of life and learning.

They believed that the true college of liberal arts was not supposed to give a student his philosophy, history, literature and science as unrelated intellectual exercises at random; they were supposed to leave him with a sound interpretation of his own experience and of the world in which he lived. That is why the integrative principle in those days was to be found in the strong emphasis placed on theology and scholastic philosophy.

Such in brief were the schools of the old Society prior to its suppression in 1773, and those of the restored Society as well, from 1814 almost down to the turn of the present century.

Meanwhile, however, the Protestant idea of higher education was changing radically all around them. "Papists" and "heretics" had entered the American field together in 1636. In fact, a few months after the Pilgrim Fathers had begun a school in Newtown, Massachusetts, which was later to be known as Harvard, the Jesuit Fathers began one at Newtown, Maryland. As Msgr. Peter Guilday once pointed out at Georgetown, the first took for its motto "Christo et Ecclesiae," the second "Ad Majorem Dei Gloriam," and both sought to carry on the Renaissance tradition, derived by Harvard from Cambridge in England, by the Jesuits from the University of Paris. They were not in the beginning as different, or as unequal as might be supposed at this late date.

The development of Jesuit schools in the United States had from the first paralleled the development of the country, even in its picturesque details. In Colonial days, the Jesuits were Colonials but second class citizens, subject to the penal laws of Britain. There was less persecution of individuals than in England. No one was hanged, drawn and quartered for going to Mass, but chapels and schools were at the mercy of the dominant church group, and Jesuits were an easy target. After the Revolution, Georgetown, with its dignified little buildings of red and white, was the kind of place a man like George Washington would select for his relatives and, in 1909, they used to point out the place by the Old North porch where he tethered his horse on visits to his two nephews, Bushrod and Augustine Washington, registered in 1793. In the great trek West, they wore their coonskin caps more often than birettas and St. Louis University began as a log cabin in the woods. Later they built as they could, in New England for the poor, down-trodden Irish, and in California, for the rough and enriched prospectors of gold. Gonzaga University acquired its property from the Northern Pacific Railroad in the boom days of early Spokane, and Creighton was endowed by the man who completed the overland telegraph from the Mississippi to the Pacific. In fact, until about the time of the Civil War when the modern spirit of naturalism began to take hold of the colleges of the United States, the only striking differences between a Jesuit college and its Protestant collegiate neighbors were a difference in method and a difference in dogma. Their general objective and their loyalty to their own concept of the Christian tradition were very similar. It was the infiltration of naturalism that began the great cleavage between them.

Had it not been for the insidious effects of this pervasive philosophy, the average American college would have kept its Christian outlook in spite of a variety of attacks like one that came through the lower schools as early as 1829. This minor crisis was described by Orestes Brownson at Mt. St. Mary's College on June 29, 1853 in a forgotten passage from an address to the Philomathian Society:

"It is not without design that I have mentioned the name of Frances Wright, the favorite pupil of Jeremy Bentham and famous infidel lecturer through our country, some twenty years ago; for I happen to know, what may not be known to you all, that she and her friends were the great movers in the scheme of godless education, now the fashion in our country. I knew this remarkable woman well, and it was my shame to share, for a time, many of her views, for which I ask pardon of God and of my countrymen. I was for a brief time in her confidence, and one of those selected to carry into execution her plans. The great object was to get rid of Christianity, and to convert our churches into halls of science. The plan was not to make open attacks upon religion, although we might belabor the clergy and bring them into contempt where we could; but to establish a system of state—we said national—schools, from which all religion was to be excluded, in which nothing was to be taught but such knowledge as is verifiable by the senses, and to which all parents were to be compelled by law to send their children. Our complete plan was to take the children from their parents at the age of twelve, or eighteen months, and to have them nursed, fed, clothed, and trained in these schools at the public expense; but at any rate, we were to have godless schools for all the children of the country, to which the parents would be compelled by law to send them. The first thing to be done was to get this system of schools established. For this purpose, a secret society was formed, and the whole country was to be organized somewhat on the plan of the carbonari of Italy, or as were the revolutionists throughout Europe by Bazard preparatory to the revolutions of 1820 and 1830. This organization was commenced in 1829, in the city of New York, and to my own knowledge was effected throughout a considerable part of New York State. How far it was extended in other states or whether it is still kept up I do not know, for I abandoned it in the latter part of the year 1830, and have since had no confidential relations with any engaged in it; but this much I can say, the plan has been successfully pursued, the views we put forth have gained great popularity, and the whole action of the country on the subject has taken the direction we sought to give it."

Left to itself a movement like this might have gone the way of other religious and anti-religious crusades of the day, but about the time Brownson was delivering his lecture over a hundred years ago, Europe was stirring with another brand new system of thought which happened to have been popular in Ionia six hundred years before Christ. Its champion in philosophy was Comte; in science, Darwin; in education, Spencer; in literature, Balzac. They each had a different approach, but their conclusions were the same: nature is the source of all, all is explained by nature because there is no reason to suppose the existence of the supernatural or the spiritual. This philosophy, when imported into the United States by our own native scholars who had flocked to Paris and Berlin for the doctorate, robbed our essentially religious colleges of their basic substance. Gradually, as they became non-sectarian and finally secular, the classical Christian tradition of the liberal arts merged imperceptibly into the liberal humanistic tradition, if we may borrow the terminology of Sir Walter Moberley (*The Crisis of the University*) before it became completely submerged in the technological democratic ideal.

Naturalism was already far advanced at the turn of the century due largely to the immense prestige of the great Charles Eliot of Harvard. After forty years he was still president in 1909 and ranked with Oliver Wendell Holmes as one of the major deities in the intellectual life of America. He taught that the religion of the future was the service of mankind, a service based on actual experience and analyzed by the scientific attitude of mind. Having thus efficiently helped to change the substance of higher education in America, this distinguished chemist and university president turned his attention to its form. For years scholars had accepted, almost without question, the practice of demanding that the student achieve competence in the wisdom studies, as they were called, the liberal studies, philosophy, literature, history and pure science, in order to qualify for a college degree. Practically all the courses were prescribed and the student was exposed to an intellectual discipline that was uniform and traditional. Today we are ready to admit that the old program was too rigid and too narrow, but we cannot join Dr. Eliot's many admirers when they maintain that he had to go too far in order to loosen the strangle hold of the past. For the extreme electivism which he did not originate, but did so much to popularize, knocked the form out of a college education which had already lost its substance. It only remained then for some brilliant young professors at Columbia, like Edward L. Thorndike, William H. Kilpatrick and John Dewey to change its direction, and that they were already beginning to do in 1909.

This turmoil and the subsequent confusion were not lost even on a rather scatter-brained Freshman. He had seen his older brothers floundering at Yale, Brown, Lafayette and Columbia, and although he was confident that he was getting more than they got, he was vaguely conscious that even the Jesuits at Georgetown had not been unaffected by the educational atmosphere. Much later in life it seemed to him that, some time after 1895, the pressure had become so strong that the Fathers of the Society of Jesus in this country began a series of critical compromises. He did not say that they were not wise or necessary, but merely that they were critical.

They not only abandoned their traditional six year program for the "Four—Four," but began to expand the old "erudition" into separate courses and even departments. Latin and Greek remained as strict entrance requirements and the Bachelor of Arts was still the normal goal, but an ever increasing number of students from non-Jesuit schools was changing the avowed scope of Belles Lettres or Freshman as it was now called and even of Rhetoric or Sophomore making it necessary to squander college time on the drilling once confined to the old grammar grades. The B.S., and in some places the Ph.B., had been introduced but even those who graduated Bachelors of Arts had not quite what their predecessors had been given a decade before.

There were other factors too, which contributed to

the difficulty of the situation. Their old competitors, once on a more even basis with them, had already received rich endowments and had reason to anticipate fabulous gifts from the new class of multi-millionaires that came into being after the Civil War. Harvard in 1900 had $11,766,370, equivalent today to $40,-000,000. Yale had $5,000,000, and Princeton more than $2,000,000. But except for Creighton in the Middle West, which started with $150,000, the Jesuits had received practically nothing. Catholics for the most part had little to give and with their little were busy building parishes, hospitals, orphan asylums and seminaries. As a consequence their colleges had no endowments whatever except "living endowments," the name given to contributed services, and the Jesuit buildings which in 1850 had seemed elegant to the Yale professor were by 1900 quite inadequate. About that time too, their men stopped going to Europe for their training and were not properly prepared for all the new specialized courses they were supposed to give. As an end result of these circumstances they went through a transition period of about ten years which they do not recall with too much pride.

By 1909 however Jesuit colleges were beginning to emerge from the confusion. Their compromises were beginning to work. It could not be said even then that the *Ratio Studiorum* was strictly observed but enough was left to keep the conservatives relatively quiet while the door was being opened to a generation which was not prepared for and did not want a typically Jesuit education or even the liberal arts course known as Nineteenth Century American.

What profit then did a Georgetown student of 50 years ago derive from his exposure to the liberal arts? His arts course was a substantial one. He was offered, besides elementary theology, universal history, and mathematics, a year of poetry and a year of rhetoric, both of them studied in Latin and Greek and English, two years of scholastic philosophy with inorganic chemistry, mechanics, physics and just a soupçon of geology and astronomy thrown in. Some of the science, physics in particular, was taught with enthusiasm but none with any laboratory periods, and evening sessions at the old telescope in the observatory were on the informal side. Electives were such that after the passage of half a century, he is not quite clear on the subject matter but has a vague impression that one was called political economy.

What vitalized this course for him was a glorious Summer in Europe at the end of his Freshman year.

With two of his classmates he rode the highways and byways of the Continent from Naples to Paris, some 1540 miles on a bicycle, crossing the Alps at the Brenner Pass. It was the Europe of 1870–1914. Four years later it had vanished and another and yet another took its place.

Then too Washington itself was no small help as a background for the liberal arts. It gave our undergraduate a chance to meet interesting people, attend White House receptions, and important sessions of Congress; sample the social life of the city which was still conservative, see everything that was worth while in the theatre, and hear a lot of good music. One night he watched President Taft leaning far over the box, applauding in ecstasy when Tetrazzini finished for the third time his favorite aria—the Polonaise from *Mignon*. Four years of all this and he was conscious that, while expert in nothing, he had come to like a lot of things that were worth liking, and that at twenty there was still time to learn a trade.

Instead of a trade however, there was something else in store for him. By the end of his Junior year it became evident that left to himself he would never amount to very much, but that as a small cell in a great body he might be able to justify his existence.

So without the slightest enthusiasm, in fact with something pretty close to natural repugnance, he decided to offer himself as a candidate to the Society of Jesus. To the surprise of everyone who knew him, he was accepted and after graduating without distinction left for the Novitiate.

II

In a Coonskin Coat

IN JULY OF 1919 our Georgetown Bachelor of Arts who had been so mildly interested in education, but had nevertheless cast in his lot with the Jesuits in 1913, came back to the world after six wonderful years in a cocoon.

These years had not been wasted. He had learned a number of things. He could meditate now, scrub floors, read spiritual books, and say *no* to himself. Moreover his intellectual motivation had been stepped up. After a year spent reviewing the classics, he was a little more at home with Horace and Homer than had seemed previously possible. Three more years of scholastic philosophy and another look at Chemistry and Physics, with just a dash of educational methods, had transformed him into a very much interested pedagogue, a "Scholastic" about to begin his "Regency."

This period of teaching in a young Jesuit's life is designed chiefly for his own benefit and only secondarily for the benefit of the school. After six or seven years in the rarefied atmosphere of the cloister, three or four years of contact with the next generation is just the training necessary to send him back to his theology and ordination, a well-rounded adult. Of course he does fully as much for the school as the school does for him. He brings, together with his inexperience, an enthusiasm and freshness that inspire the students in his classes and keep Jesuit colleges from becoming treadmills. He is of course profoundly conscious of the embarrassing mistakes that have been made by previous generations and realizes that the world is waiting for the right answers, which he is not at all unwilling to give. The inevitable compromises that follow the resistance of the older men tend to preserve the best of what has been while adding just enough of what is to come.

Our Regent, the title of a teaching Scholastic, was not however as impatient with the legacy of the past as many of his successors have been and are today. He could see that too much of the past was gone already. He found on his arrival at Fordham that, during his absence from the world, a great deal had vanished besides three Empires, most notably perhaps the old feeling of permanence. That very summer, for example, the allies changed their minds about Czarist Russia and in September began a withdrawal from their White Sea camp. In a few months Admiral Kolchack would be shot by the Bolsheviki. Some experts confidently predicted that the Reds could not stay in power five years, but the non-experts were inclined to be skeptical. On the home front Prohibition had been slipped over quietly on a free and careless people so that the bright lexicon of youth had already been enriched with such invaluable terms as jazz, flapper, bootlegger, speakeasy and racketeer. It was the year of the ill-starred League of Nations. Wilson's fourteen points had been mauled beyond recognition before the Treaty of Versailles had been signed, and during the first week of class the President became mysteriously ill.

There was every reason for anxiety among the educators of the country but the general atmosphere of irrational optimism was infectious and colleges were not worried about their problems. As a nation, we had just made the world safe for democracy. We had conquered the only bad people in existence, and war was once more over forever. We saw more clearly than before that man's purpose in life, especially here in America, was his own health, culture and comfort. The post-war boom was gathering momentum and would never slow down again. Recessions were a thing of the past, so that our intellectuals had nothing more serious on their minds than the current urge to educate the masses for leisure.

During the war the Government had taken over a large number of colleges and universities as training centers for the Army and Navy, and although then, as more recently, the institutions stated with dignity that they were always glad to make financial sacrifices for their country, most of them emerged with their debts paid and a quantity of useful buildings and surplus property. This marked the beginning of a great hand-out, the end of which no man can foretell.

For the faculty, however, it meant the end of touring the country in search, if not of college material, at least of high school graduates who could pay their tuition. Boys who before 1915 had never thought of themselves in terms of a campus had felt the thrill of strolling in uniform from Vanderbilt Hall to the Alumni Stadium, and as a consequence were never to be quite the same again. Returning to private life, nothing would do for themselves and their younger brothers but more and greener ivy. Registrations boomed all over the country, money rolled in, and everything began to flourish except the liberal arts.

Unfortunately the program of general education had begun to disintegrate under our eyes into an elaborate series of pre-professional courses; pre-law, pre-medicine (at that time two years was enough for either), pre-dental (one year would do), pre-business, pre-podiatry—most of it looking to information, facts, dollars and cents, too little of it helping the student to see life steadily and see it whole, to see life and live life as the great men before us had lived it and seen it—*mutatis mutandis*, of course. Some things in life have to change and should change. Subjects for example, problems, and activities should change. But sound ideas and quality should abide, and it seemed to a young teacher after the First World War that ideas and quality were changing most of all.

Old Doctor Charles Eliot was still alive and listened to attentively, though long since a president emeritus. When he relinquished his post to Abbot Lawrence Lowell in 1910, Harvard with expressions of profound admiration for the champion of electivism had started an immediate if orderly retreat from his most beloved innovation. This retreat took the now familiar form of introducing a modicum of unity through fields of concentration, and when this was combined at length with the reintroduction of general education (a term that was preferred to liberal education) for first and second years, everyone knew that the old electivism at Harvard had been canonically exorcised if not decently interred. But meanwhile the influence had gone out in concentric circles, and the further it travelled the more fantastic the results became. By 1919 it had reached the farthest shore and an amazing number of colleges were run on the straight cafeteria plan. The country was full of cold-blooded emporiums selling chunks of dead and unrelated information for seven dollars a pound; two semester hours of *je ne sais quoi* for fifteen dollars.

More significant still was the dominant position of Columbia's controversial Teacher's College where the Four Horsemen of the Apocalypse were interpreting for America the naturalism of the nineteenth century.

The nineteenth century is mentioned not because naturalism was peculiar to that period, but because it has had such a long and disreputable history that some limitation is necessary. Naturalism, as we have already suggested is essentially a twofold denial; a denial of the supernatural and a denial of the spiritual. It is usually referred to as secularism and defined as "a form of opinion which concerns itself only with questions, the issue of which can be tested by the experience of this life," but in practice it is an effort to degrade man to the level of mockingbirds and rain; to wipe out, as the expression goes, all discontinuity in nature. Through it, according to de Hovre, "Man's mental life is reduced to psychology, psychology to physiology, physiology to biology, and biology to mechanism . . . Concepts become percepts; ideas become images; intelligence becomes a function of the brain. The soul is reduced to matter, the will is identified with instinct, and freedom yields to determinism."

From the middle of the nineteenth century the dominance of this naturalistic philosophy, whether with a shade of difference it preferred to call itself secularism, positivism, scientism, or just old-fashioned materialism, appeared in all departments of life; in science, art, history, religion, and conspicuously in education.

As Von Humboldt used to say, "Whatever we wish to see introduced into the life of a nation, must be first introduced into its schools," and the great introducer in this case was Herbert Spencer. When he wrote that "to prepare us for complete living is the function which education has to discharge," you might think he was quoting from a stock commencement address by the President of Boston College, but his complete living is not the only one. Scholastics still sit in the back of the hall and exchange knowing glances, when the Rector says with feeling that "Jesuit education aims to train the whole man." Everybody claims today that his own particular educational system seeks to develop the well-rounded man, but they are not always talking about the same curves. Spencer thought only of complete living here. "What knowledge is of most worth?" he asked. "Science. For direct self-preservation, or the maintenance of life and health, the all important knowledge is—science. For that indirect self-preservation which we call gaining a livelihood, the knowledge of greatest value is —science. For that interpretation of national life, past and present, without which a citizen cannot regulate his life, the indispensable key is—science. And for the purpose of discipline, whether intellectual, moral or religious, the most efficient study is once more— science."

How much this naturalism was affecting our education after World War I was shown by the fact that science gradually became the main instrument of education in the United States. It began to dehumanize the American schools. As Max Scheler put it in *Person und Sache*, "There is no point perhaps on which modern minds are more in accord than on this one, namely, that nature and machinery, things which man should control, have come to dominate man more and more; that things are becoming more powerful, more beautiful, more noble, and that man is constantly becoming smaller and more insignificant, a mere cog in the machine he has built."

Since nature was the only reality, the study of nature—that is, the physical sciences—became the principal, indeed the only genuine source of knowledge. Of all the physical sciences none fascinated the educators of the '20s like biology with its tremendous social implications. Biological psychology hit the Teachers Colleges with full force only in the '30s, but already three generations had fought the good fight on the lines laid down by Charles Darwin in *The Origin of Species* and *The Descent of Man*. Now William H. Kilpatrick, one of the Four Horsemen we mentioned, could write with truth, "It seems not too much to say that the foremost task of thought during recent decades has been to elaborate the implications of this doctrine." His favorite implication overemphasized the confusion and mutability of the universe.

Everything was presented as in flux, so that no conclusions about anything in the social, economic, or ethical order could be more than tentative.

Dr. Kilpatrick's colleague, the great John Dewey, who had by now successfully linked American education with positivistic sociology, had every reason to regard himself as a complete success. The educational trend was already clear. Within another ten years, he would be able to say that he had remade our schools in his own image and likeness. The effect of his teaching was chiefly at the grade and secondary levels, but the reverberations echoed in many a college and university classroom, so that in 1919 all educational and philosophical circles admitted that John Dewey was a force that could not be ignored. With his so-called activity program we could feel some sympathy. The old *Ratio Studiorum* prescribed somewhat the same process. A student learned drama by writing a play, or at least by carrying a spear. Our young regent did not feel that he had capitulated to the spirit of Teachers College when he organized in 1921 a playshop where students could write and produce their own plays. The one-act play, a novelty at the time, was an admirable instrument for making a young author feel equally close to Euripides and O'Henry. In the same venerable tradition, the Sopho-

more learned rhetoric by making a speech, and dia-
lectics by lively disputation. He was encouraged to
build model bridges and catapults, and to sing Greek
choruses and the marching songs of the Roman le-
gionaries. But that was as far as the Jesuits cared to
go. They were unprepared to follow the new prophet
in scrapping books and lectures and in sneering at formal learning, or what he called with contempt "The
Funded Capital of Civilization." They had had some
experience with the self-directed spontaneous activity
of children and feared the worst when they saw the
little threats turned loose. They were even reactionary enough to believe that the teacher also had a right
to life, liberty and the pursuit of happiness. Equally
disturbing to these conservatives in the early '20s was
the rejection on the part of the Deweyites of all the
external compulsions of authority, especially of penal-
ties and awards. In the schools of those days, the last
thing in the world the liberals seemed to want was
order. It may have been a matter of sour grapes, but
they certainly made a virtue of their necessity. In this
their policy conformed to the general theory that the
schools should keep pace with society and not vice
versa. Their symbol should be a mirror not a torch, as
the traditionalists tried with some difficulty to maintain. The logical conclusion seemed to say that the

more chaotic society might become, the more chaotic the schools should be. The slogan seemed to be "Let us have less effort and more joy," unmindful of the fact that true joy lies in well ordered effort and happiness in self control. Like his activity program, John Dewey's stress on the necessity of constant experiment was good to a degree, but overdone. He would have us scrap the past altogether, and start each morning as if it were the morning of creation. So too with his pragmatism. Up to a point utility is a reasonable guide, but when it becomes the only norm of value the conclusions can be completely preposterous. So too with his socialism. We are, all of us, out for socialism of a kind. The modern Popes in their encyclicals urge us to work incessantly for the good of society, but Prof. Dewey went all the way, making society his god, maintaining that man lives in, for and by society.

Thus it would be misleading to rail against the Godless education of the 1920s. It wasn't godless at all. All the great men who gave us what we had in our American schools worshipped gods without exception. Some of them worshipped the one true God, some had fashioned their own. According to Jacques Maritain, "For Spencer [God] was nature. For Comte, humanity; for Rousseau, liberty; for Freud, sex; for

Durkheim and Dewey, society; for Wundt, culture; for Emerson, the individual." Furthermore, these objects of their devotion were all good in themselves, as gold and wood and stone are good. It was only man's adoration that made them evil things, that made them the strange gods forbidden by the first Commandment; frivolous gods, like those on Mount Olympus; impotent gods that had no power to lift man higher than himself. And after World War I man needed a lift.

Young as he was and temperamentally eager for experiment, a scholastic of 1919 could not help looking over his shoulder at the receding past and the old liberal arts that were receding with it. So many philosophical influences were at work against the spirit of humanism that it was not immediately clear how deeply certain popular influences were affecting the situation. One of the principal intrusions of the nonacademic world came through its preoccupation with big-time college athletics. It was the era of the coonskin coat.

The purpose of sport and its place in education had always been recognized since the Golden Age of Athens. The old ideal of the *mens sana in corpore sano* had been stressed in Jesuit Schools from the 16th Century on, and even today when most of the extravagance has retired beyond the Appalachians, athletic prowess is one of the qualities we like to find in the perfect college man. But the monstrous emphasis placed on all sports and particularly on football after the first world war, was an important phenomenon in American life and cannot be ignored in any discussion of the gradual disappearance of the liberal arts. This is not to suggest that the over-stressed athlete was a complete novelty in the '20s. He could have been observed at close range ten years before, when his means of support remained a deep secret between the student treasurer of the A. A. who carried the black satchel home from the ticket office, and the student president. But all such operations at that early period were on a scale of petty larceny. It was only after the Treaty of Versailles that the operation came of age. There then appeared in many Colleges a tendency to hand the whole amazing transaction over to the alumni so that the faculty might remain pure if not in the sight of God, at least in their own. Some of the athletes employed were really College material interested in their own education and a credit then and later to their Alma Mater. For them, their duties with the squad were on a business basis and brought them scholastic advantages which they could not otherwise have enjoyed. There were

too many others, however, before the days of the
post-season games, who were known as turkeys because they were so apt to vanish at Thanksgiving.
This practical interpretation of the residence requirements was not confined to football. There was
for example one center of learning in 1920 that took
up big-time ice hockey on the suggestion of an undergraduate enthusiast who offered to produce an entire team forthwith. The players arrived overnight
from Montreal, spent a day getting used to their new
names, played a five game schedule with conspicuous
success, and then entrained once more for Canada,
none the poorer though none the wiser, for their
brush with higher education. It was all part of the
crazy coonskin decade of course, but lingered on unfortunately even after the financial crash had ended
some of the other aberrations of the times. The
Carnegie investigation of athletics was overdue, but
underdone. Notorious transgressors slipped through
the net, and the outcry died down once more as it
always does.

The effect of this curious tribal weakness on the
liberal arts was indirect but noticeable. In cases
where the athletes remained even after the season
was over, some sort of provision had to be made for
them. Thucydides and Plato were not too popular,

the physical sciences had an awkward way of running laboratories in the afternoons and there was no point whatever in scheduling higher mathematics. Some centers of learning were smart enough to solve the problem by offering degrees in Physical Education and were subsequently able to advertise with loud-speakers that the entire backfield was maintaining a B average. Others further developed the old Ph.B. and the new B.S.II.

This latter plan had the additional advantage of providing for the pampered sons of potential benefactors but attracted too many students who could have taken the traditional A.B. degree or a good B.S.I with a reasonable amount of effort. As will appear later however, this B.S.II with majors in English, Spanish and the Social Sciences proved to be far from an unmixed evil for the Jesuit Colleges themselves, and was in any case inevitable if they were to serve the growing needs of the country and the Church. It was not merely that non-Jesuit high schools were already far from the old tradition that prescribed four years of Latin and three of Greek, but even our own high schools, which furnished an ever diminishing minority of candidates, were changing rapidly too.

While the reorganization at the turn of the cen-

tury had created a degree of confusion, Jesuit high
schools were finding themselves again by 1909, and
the results they were achieving were not too unlike
those of an earlier and a brighter day. But beginning
with the First World War, they were forced to accept
against their better judgment a variety of diet which
resulted in graduating from the preparatory school
too many boys who were not prepared; too many boys
who could not properly read a book; who could not
write a correct English paragraph; who could not
translate a sentence, ancient or modern, into good
English; who could not solve a simple problem in
algebra, or even arithmetic, and who therefore, no
matter what assorted tidbits they may have picked
up in civics, sociology, chemistry, carpentry, music
appreciation and hygiene, were not prepared to take
advantage of the liberal arts.

It is true, and it may be added in all humility, that
in preserving at least some of the ancient discipline of
Latin and Greek with a method of teaching them that
had the advantage of long experience, the Jesuit
schools did escape the ultimate in chaos, but they
must confess to a certain nostalgia at times when they
look back on the days before the pressure became too
great, before the preparatory idea became complicated by the terminal idea, back to the days when

they were satisfied to give their boys what they considered sound and essential training for college. It was a simple thing that they tried to give them, merely a habit of study, the power of correct expression, a firm grip on elementary mathematics and grasp enough of another language, preferably Latin, to begin in Freshman a serious study of its literature. It was very simple, but they are still looking for something better.

This high school problem was a constant source of anxiety to our young regent because after a preliminary year with the graduating class of Fordham Prep, he had been assigned to teach Latin, Greek and English to college Freshmen from fourteen different high schools. As it happened that was the last year that Fordham retained the old Jesuit system of one teacher for the three branches, and he had a chance to compare it with the departmental system which was introduced the next September. His verdict was that, given the right teacher, the old system was preferable. It made for unity of impression, orderliness, and proportion. Given the wrong teacher, it was an injustice to thirty students, and as the registration expanded, the chance of injustice increased as it became more and more difficult to find teachers who could do well in three languages. On the division of courses, the two Fathers got the Greek and Latin, while the scholastic was assigned the literature that was the easiest of the three to read but the most difficult of the three to teach, English. It was the most difficult subject he ever had to teach. Greek and Philosophy were easy by comparison, almost as easy as Geometry. Fortunately it was possible by close team work to coordinate the material with the Latin and Greek being taught to the same classes. But one could easily see how the new system might weaken the unity of impression expected from the liberal arts.

One light there was in the increasing confusion of the 1920s, and that came from the rise of the accrediting associations, national, regional and state. The earliest form of educational supervision in this country developed from an act of the Legislature of the State of New York in 1784, in vesting the Regents of the University of the State of New York with all the former rights and privileges of Kings College (thereafter to be known as Columbia) and granting them the power to found and endow Schools and Colleges anywhere in the State and to hold them subject to their direction and visitation. In 1895, the qualifications of a Georgetown student who had applied for the Columbia Medical School were questioned and this led to the earliest recorded examination of Ford-

[47]

ham and St. Francis Xavier with flattering results. Meantime an accrediting association had been established in New England (1885) and this was followed by the Middle States Association, the North Central and Southern Associations. But it was only after the First World War that the schools in the East took their Associations very seriously.

The weaker institutions, who saw in their activities a deep and sinister plot, would soon denounce them, but in time these backward high schools and colleges were ready to admit that they would never have pulled themselves together without the pressure of inspection by unprejudiced strangers. Most of them recently had been content to admit more students than they could educate and were inclined to attribute their sudden and welcome expansion to their own intrinsic excellence. Too many failed to realize what serious problems were involved in staffing and equipping a modern college. Their catalogues were spangled with brand new science courses, but their laboratories and faculties were often of the Ming dynasty. In some cases the libraries, usually open for an hour after lunch, were fantastically inadequate. There was one college, for example, which in 1920 allowed the football team to run up a debt of sixty-five thousand dollars, equivalent today to nearly two hundred thousand dollars, while the total library expenses for the same year, including the purchase and repair of books, salaries, magazines and equipment, came to three hundred eighty-five dollars and seventy-five cents. This is not an exaggeration. When criticized, delinquents of this kind defended themselves by sneering at the importance of equipment. They were never done repeating Garfield's famous tribute to Mark Hopkins but unfortunately, while there was no dearth of logs on which the ideal student might sit, it was rare indeed that he had found an ideal teacher on the other end. For such institutions as these, and there were too many, the rise of accreditation was an incalculable blessing. Of course it had its bad features, as well. In the beginning, there was too much stress on the quantitative, too little on the qualitative. The examiners were apparently more interested in the number of books in the library and the amount of money spent than in the selection of titles. So too, with the number of offerings in the catalogues and the number of Ph.D.s on the staff. The result was in the first few years an indiscriminate compliance with mechanical regulations. Tons of Government publications were put on the shelves and even old telephone books were made available "for population research" in the new soci-

ology department. As for the traffic in graduate degrees, they took on rush-hour proportions. After a few
years, however, the associations clarified their own
thinking and today come as close as may be to a
sound qualitative judgment.

Their principal contribution was not so much the
part they played in eliminating many diploma mills,
as the help they gave to colleges that had a real function to fulfill but were handicapped by poverty or
inexperience. Catholics were convinced that they had
to get an enormous job done in a very short time and
the path they blazed for themselves in toil and anxiety
was marked here and there with the ruins of a high
school or a college which had been built with too
much enthusiasm. Between 1786 and 1850 the Jesuits,
whose numbers were still small, founded or took over
16 Colleges and Universities for men. Only 6 of these
are still in existence: Georgetown, St. Louis, Spring
Hill, Xavier (Cincinnati), Fordham and Holy Cross.
Up to the present, 30 of their schools have disappeared in various parts of the United States—beginning with Newtown Manor School, closed by the
Puritans in 1659, and coming down to St. John's University, Toledo which was taken over by the diocese
in 1936. In some cases, through no fault of their own,
the neighborhood changed or the city declined. In

some cases it was a matter of bad judgment. In some cases it was the result of operating too close to the subsistence level. For example, for the first fifty years of its life (1841–1891), Fordham's gifts averaged about $2,000 a year. With all due allowance for "the ideal teacher on the end of a log," this institution, typical of so many, was making its "ideal teachers" teach five hours a day, supervise the yard, prefect the dormitories and put on the College play, while the lay teachers were simply the best who could be found for twenty-five dollars a month and board. That such struggling colleges were what they were in 1919 would have been a moral miracle if there had been no compensating sources of power. As it was, they had what it always takes to succeed in any sphere: self-sacrificing and forgotten men who quietly gave the best years of their lives to build up the bodies, sharpen the minds, refine the tastes and soften the hearts of the boys who came to them so that their lives might be full lives, and their ultimate success assured; dedicated scholars, clerical and lay, who were never distracted by professional will o' the wisps, who for years beyond remembering had watched the rise and fall of every theory of education which began by ignoring man's fundamental nature and supernatural end.

[51]

The fact remains, however, that the Jesuit institutions were always part of the national picture and influenced by national trends. So in the period under discussion, they reflected to some extent most of the unfortunate changes going on around them. Like most of their neighbors, they also took too many applicants, too many of them poorly trained. They also were tempted to under-emphasize the arts and pure science. They also organized courses for new degrees which they deliberately tempered to the shorn lamb (who was later to be covered with a sheepskin) so that sometimes they had to acknowledge as alumni together with their stars men whose grasp of the vernacular was uncertain, and who admitted that they had not read a book since graduation. They also succumbed in varying degrees to the coonskin propaganda that high-power athletics were essential to an institution's prestige and financial success. The time came when they even found themselves fighting to keep out of their schools the insidious effects of the naturalism that was rampant around them. In some parts of the battle line they seemed to be losing ground, but when the '20s had spent themselves, they still had enough of their old tradition left to rank as defenders of the liberal arts.

UNIVERSITY OF CAMBRIDGE

FOUNDED A.D. 915

III

In an English Fog

IT WAS DOUBLY INTERESTING THEN to go over to Europe in the middle '20s and see how our British cousins once removed were meeting the problem created everywhere for the liberal arts by the post-war adjustment.

On a previous visit during the reign of Edward VII, the Empire had seemed indestructable. Toynbee could probably have detected seeds of disintegration all over the place as he did in the Rome of Augustus, but to an American boy of 14 she was still first among the powers of the world, and though he was fond of giving a *Pinafore* twist to the famous last line,

"Britons never never never shall be slaves. What? Never?," he had to admit in 1907 that the sun was still trying unsuccessfully to set on the Union Jack. The German challenge was already in the planning stage but the Empire was rich, proud, secure and immutable, like her navy, her royal family, her four banks and her two universities.

Twenty years later, she was poor, shaken and wondering about tomorrow. It was not a state of merely temporary embarrassment, financial or political. It was a state of readjustment to a permanently lower level. The dislike for Americans expressed just then with brutal frankness by the upper classes was a byproduct of her insecurity and wounded pride. Of course our fellow countrymen were not entirely blameless. It was one thing for a New Yorker to thrill with ecstasy on reaching home after an exile of a few months and whisper to his closest friends what a gorgeous thing it is to live in a place that pulsates with the beauty of power and freshness and life, but it was unpardonable to tell Englishmen who had been raised on what Dr. Johnson said about the traffic at Charing Cross that the London of 1927 was an ugly depressing town with the odor of death in the streets. And yet Americans were just blunt and thoughtless enough to say things like that. Most of them had the curious feeling, in the larger English cities, that they were back in the year of Our Lord 1902, and there is always something sad and musty about the immediate past. Riding in a sedan chair or a Roman chariot is a lark, but the sight of an old Pierce Arrow is poignant. It is like an early picture of Ethel Barrymore. If Americans insisted on feeling this way about the modern centers of England, they should have kept the conversation on the lovely little villages of thatched houses that were still crowding contentedly at the feet of incredible old parish churches, or better still on Oxford and Cambridge—or best of all just on Cambridge.

Great changes had undoubtedly occurred even along the Cam since 1914. Thackeray, who once occupied the same rooms in Trinity which he afterwards assigned to Pendennis, would in 1927 have rubbed his eyes in amazement. He and his friends whom he met in the hall every night for dinner—Alfred and Charles Tennyson, Edward Fitzgerald and Hallam, and Spedding and Monckton Mills—would have agreed that the hall was unchanged and the buttery and the Great Court and the Backs, but what had happened to the university?

In the middle '20s it was just recovering from the War and working out the practical recommendations of a Royal Commission. This had been appointed by the Crown when the University Senate discovered that the budget could no longer be balanced without a government subsidy—an ominously modern discovery. Its work was concluded in a spirit of harmony and already steps had been taken to make the university more efficient and more accessible to the general public. Still, compared with one of our own educational centers, even the oldest, it was delightfully medieval.

An American Cantab visiting Oxford about this time grew weary of the invariable question put to him: "Which do you like better, Oxford or Cambridge?" He made history by answering: "Oxford, of course. Cambridge is too full of associations and memories. It hasn't an up-and-going factory within a hundred miles and the college buildings are centuries behind the times. Oxford is more like Chicago."

What made this loyalty to the past more striking was the great university's wide reputation for science and mathematics. It was better known in America for the Cavendish laboratories than for King's College Chapel—but its history was really a history of the liberal arts. In the days of St. Thomas More, Cambridge was warmer to the new learning than Oxford and the tower in old Queens College where Erasmus

spent so many irascible years will always be a picturesque symbol of her devotion to Latin and Greek.

In the first place it was never too large. Larger than
Oxford, it was in the nineteen twenties about half
the size of Fordham. Its undergraduates were moreover divided among twenty-one colleges in groups
small enough to be on easy terms with their own
masters, their tutors and most of the bright lights
lecturing in their particular tripos. This tripos was
not a department but a curriculum which took its
name from the three-legged stools on which the clerks
of Chaucer's time used to sit when they were not off
looking for trouble in Trumpington. At first glance,
it might seem that spending three years on one three-
legged stool should not be commended as preparation
for a Bachelor's degree, but of course the stools are
legendary now, and the students quite mature. The
English undergraduate is more advanced than the
Continental or even the American. An English boy
leaving Winchester or Rugby would qualify at once
for a French Baccalaureate or a B.A. in Robert Hutchins' Chicago, and after two years in the university
would be of graduate caliber.

What is more important still is the fact that a
liberal education can be built up most admirably in
the tripos tradition around any single one of the wis-

dom studies. Take, for example, the curriculum 35 years ago of an honors candidate in English. In addition to a very thorough survey of the field from Caedmon to Thomas Hardy (who was still living), and with a staggering reading list designed to use up every moment of the generous vacations, he was responsible for a great deal more than English literature. He had for example, the history of criticism, which began not with the *Ars Poetica* of Horace, or even Aristotle's *Poetics*, but with *The Clouds* and *The Frogs* of Aristophanes, and made its way down to T. S. Eliot through France and Spain and Germany as well as England. He was besides ready on a dozen masterpieces of medieval Latin, like the *Rules* of St. Benedict and the *Confessions* of St. Augustine, or on ten great books in original French and Italian. The history of tragedy took him all over civilization from the Book of Job to Ibsen, and his paper on English philosophers of the 17th century presupposed a good grasp of Locke and Hume and Hooker and Hobbs. Thus English was made to include considerable history, philosophy and languages, with more than a splash of semantics and psychology. This resulted in a rich variety without impairing the unity of the curriculum, an achievement comparable to that of the old *Ratio Studiorum* which tied in so much outside matter called "erudition" with the simple program of classics and philosophy.

In the same spirit, the form of the examination and the grading had a timelessness about them that was centuries away from a true-false or a multiple-choice. There was no such thing as answering a question correctly. There were not any questions. At the end of each part of the tripos, the Cantab was allowed to write 18 half-hour essays at high speed, expressing his opinions with regard to various phases of the matter suggested by the examiner. He was graded on the solidity and maturity of his opinions, the evidence of wide reading, and the quality of his style. Of course you could trust the undergraduates to find a don's weakness, and experience had taught them that their examiners were always impressed by a lavish use of apt quotations preferably in various languages, so that meeting afterwards on the steps of the Senate House, one would call out to another: "I got up 26 quotes and used 18. One was in Tamil. I had to swat frightfully."

Another factor making for an impressive sense of order and direction in the Cambridge of those days was the attitude of the student body itself toward study. Considerably less than a third was ineligible for honors, and the colleges were reluctant to accept a pass student without a very special reason. They might take, for example, a viscount's son provided he could get by the "little go," or a backward relative of the vice chancelor's mother, or occasionally the scion of a good county family. It was even suspected that the Master of St. Catherine's (or Cat's for short) was handing out athletic scholarships to a few in whom (I quote from an Oxford document of the 14th century) "the energies of their stomachs exceeded those of their minds." It was felt however that such worthies might profit by three years of ragging on Market Hill and bumping on the Cam and dancing on the Backs at Mayweek, as well as by the still more ancient custom of being smoked at in the tutor's room. But the bulk of the students were expected to be more or less interested in their own intellectual development, and one of the reasons why the conservatives looked with alarm on the new Government subsidy, was the fact that through these nondescript Members of Parliament whose votes meant so much to the university budget, some draper's son might eventually worm his way into a pass degree—something that had not happened since the time of Henry VII.

By the end of the Second World War the editor of the *Cambridge Journal* was bitter about subsequent developments. "In the past," wrote Michael Oake-shott, "a rising class was aware of something valuable enjoyed by others which it wished to share but this is not so today. The leaders of the rising class are consumed with contempt for everything which does not spring from their own desires. Their aim is loot, to appropriate to themselves . . . the shell of the institution and convert it to their own purposes." In 1927 however this was not evident. There were already, it is true, many accents heard in the courts and even in the Combination Rooms where the graduates gathered after dinner, which were certainly not accents from the public schools, but "the better sort" still made their influence felt and that in spite of the fact that the proletarian brains of the aristocracy were frequently gathered in the pass course where they could do little damage to the scholarship of their alma mater. Actually they could be of some assistance, serving to lighten the overhead and decorating the register, if not with honors, then with honorables. On the other hand, the aristocratic brains of the proletariat were already competing with similar brains of every other class for the leadership of what was still a considerable empire. One undergraduate expressed the common attitude toward success in study when he said: "If I get a first class, I shall try for a Fellowship

[63]

or take government service overseas; if I get a second class, I shall teach in the secondary schools; if I get a third class, I shall take a living in the Church." Men who received a pass degree could look forward to nothing higher than collecting rents on their own estates or some day speaking in the House of Lords.

This traditional prestige for academic accomplishment, was further buttressed by pitiless and enduring publicity. The *Times* of London ("Are there any other *Times?*"), which normally printed only four pages of news including the Court Calendar and the sermons of the Dean of St. Paul's, always found space to publish the results of the Honors exams in Oxford and Cambridge. The name of every honors undergraduate with the grade he received was read at the breakfast tables all over the empire, and his success or failure never forgotten by his friends or by his enemies. There were cases of men disqualified for modest positions in later life because thirty years before they had received a third-class in the history tripos, while in the obituaries of the Great, Generals, Right Honorables, and even Most Noble Lords, there was always room to record with pride not only that they had been wranglers in their Cambridge days or even senior optimes, but that they had captained the Hare and Hounds.

In some ways our American Jesuit though recently ordained got the impression at Cambridge that he was no longer quite adult. When he called on the Master of Christ's for the first time, "Daddy" McLean looked at the applicant's 14-year-old College records in complete bewilderment and wanted to know if all this elaborate business of semester hours and credits and grades meant that he had finished in the first-third of his class. Reassured on this essential detail by a mere nod, he examined the Master of Arts diploma from Woodstock College and asked without turning a hair if the candidate wished to try for a Doctor's or a Bachelor's degree. Having a few conservative ideas of his own about the liberal arts and some knowledge of the local tradition, the young American elected to pursue a Bachelor's leading to a Masters degree in the Honors Course. Daddy seemed relieved. It was a British choice. Very sensible.

The Ph.D. was still a recent development in England at this time, and was the subject of endless quips in public and private. Sir Arthur Quiller-Couch was never done poking fun at female students from Girton and Newnham and candidates for the Ph.D. None of the Fellows seemed to have taken the degree. There was only one lecturer in the tripos who had it. He earned just £250 a year, lived out, and saw students in a cheerless little room up two flights. (It was rumored that his family sold pianos and that he would never be elected a Fellow.) Everyone regarded a Ph.D. as a German eccentricity which for some mysterious reason interested Americans even in fields outside the physical sciences, where it might have been considered appropriate. They spoke loftily about the German ideal of scholarship as "learning more and more about less and less." To them research was not something to be done in a corner by a specialist unable to shape a literary paragraph or toss off a classical reference. It should be the more or less casual conclusion of a widely read scholar capable of announcing his discovery in heroic verse if he wanted to!

Those who braved the local prejudice and elected to pursue the Doctors degree were assigned a desk in the Library (Room Theta), and except for occasional visits to a supervisor who often as not gave the impression that the whole process was a waste of time, were adrift until they applied for examination on their submitted thesis. There were no lectures to be attended, no seminars, no term papers, no "comprehensives," no nights in "Hall," no teas with a tutor, no coffee squashes—practically no contact with the University. Everything depended on whether or not the examiners (all M.A.s) learned anything from the dissertation, and whether or not they agreed with its conclusions. There was for example one brilliant candidate at this period who was unfortunate enough to pick a subject which the dons felt they knew all about—the philosophy of John Locke—and to express certain conservative opinions which they did not happen to care for. After several failures he had to be content with the consolation degree of M. Litt. There was another, much less brilliant, candidate who was shrewd enough to pick a subject which his examiners knew very little about, *The Theological Content of the English Miracle Plays.* It gave him a chance to utilize all the courses he had taken in the seminary and he was able to dazzle these laymen with his knowledge not only of Ambrose, Augustine, and Thomas Aquinas, but even John of the Golden Mouth. They were much impressed and accorded him a kind of triumph at the first try.

This attitude of the English intellectuals toward the Ph.D. was perhaps indicative of an old prejudice in favor of Empire Products, but also of a deep conviction that Cambridge was not a brain factory but a way of life—and that intellectual development was a matter of organic growth, dependent on any number of factors. Even foreigners (for the most part "Nig-

gers," that is students from India, or "Yanks"—a term
that secessionists from South Carolina had to get
used to) were expected to adapt themselves to conditions that were as indigenous as beef and kidney pie
or the Cam itself.

Somehow one came to feel very very young in the
process. It was the Master who took you over like a
little boy to call on the "Registery" as that official was
known and it was your tutor at degree time who led
you up, holding fast to one of his proffered fingers to
the enthroned Vice Chancellor in the Senate House.
There you knelt at his feet and did homage to the
University. You became its "homo" when the Vice
Chancellor, placing his hands reverently over yours,
told you in Latin that he received you as a man of the
University, "in the Name of the Father and of the
Son and of the Holy Ghost." Meanwhile, you had submitted for a period of years to the paternal interest of
your tutor who alone could give you permission to
leave town over-night, and had jurisdiction over most
of your minor delinquencies. All the undergraduates
were compelled to wear their short academic gowns,
distinctive for each college, when they went to lectures, to Hall, to the library or to the tutor's room.
After dark, a proctor in academic dress with a buller
at his side in a top hat to do his running for him,

patrolled the streets of the town on the lookout for undergraduates who had forgotten their gowns, or had wandered absentmindedly into a pub. It was a chilling experience to be touched on the shoulder in the dark and hear a reproving voice say, "Your name and College, Sir?"

More difficult than discipline for the average American was the discovery that this business of taking a shower every time one turned around simply wasn't done. The shower was two blocks away and the traffic that had to be braved in a bathrobe and slippers was heavy with bicycles. It was much easier to have the gyp occasionally bring in a tin tub on his head and fill it before your fireplace with water heated on the hob. That explained why after a hard fought game of footer the best people could sit down at tea without a change of clothing or expression. In time, however, one thought no more of it than John Milton or Charles Robert Darwin might have thought when they too were undergraduates at Christs. In many ways time had stood so delightfully still.

Games were played as they had been for a century. Each college had its own playing fields on the outskirts of town and at two in the afternoon the roads were filled with sports-loving youngsters, each set on what pleased him most—rugby, cricket, la crosse, tennis, and some on the way to the river to row. There were no athletic dues, no scholarships (that story about Cats was whispered as a local scandal), no tickets of admission except for the rare varsity matches in London. Everyone supplied his own uniform and team expenses were met by running coffee squashes—the squash referring not to the beans but to the humans crowded in somebody's digs. Each college had a schedule of games with other colleges in every sport and nothing but undergraduate spectators were scattered all around on the grass. The mood of a cricket match was reflected in the cheering section where an enthusiast lying prone at a safe distance would look up from his Agamemnon at the crack of a bat to cry "Well held!" before returning to the second chorus. Rowing was as traditional as cricket but since the Cam was hardly wide enough, out Chesterton way, for two boats to pass unless the oars were lifted, there had grown up sometime after Alfred the Great the curious sport of bumping. No boat ever passed another. They just bumped and one dropped behind. It did seem a little frustrating but each College would turn out on bikes and on foot to keep pace along the banks cheering wildly but as ever individually, "Up Jagers!" "Forward Christs." For the annual varsity race with Oxford on the Thames, the best in

the various college crews would be selected and at
their own expense spend two weeks of vac. practicing
at Henly under a volunteer alumnus who could afford
to give two precious weeks of his time and consider
himself rewarded by the honor of assisting his alma
mater.

In Cambridge it was all part of a way of life, and
seemed essential to a liberal arts way of life. Free
afternoons were spent punting on the river, way out
of town, out through the Fens, with tea at a 15th
century inn and an hour for the book wrapped up in
your sweater, or else long trips with a "push-bike"
to Kings Lynn and the Wash where John lost his
treasure in the tide or to Ely, with its damaged but
indomitable Cathedral, or Norwich where an old
tithe barn of the 14th century had been turned into
the Maddermarket Theater. There sitting on backless
benches you could watch *Troilus and Cressida*, or
Gammer Gurton's Needle done in Elizabethan style.
Right in Cambridge there was a small theatre where
they tried everything from *Prometheus Bound* to *The
Emperor Jones*. And of course there was always the
Union down by the Bridge. In its large debate hall,
future members of Parliament learned to annihilate
their adversaries with irrelevancies. Nowhere was a
spontaneous remark so carefully groomed ahead of

time, but the overwhelming impression made on a stranger by these languid debaters draped over the speakers' stand was an extraordinary richness of background not commonly found outside of Europe. Of course the advantages of geography enjoyed by Cambridge students were shared with their French, German, and other neighbors on the Continent. Any of them could take to a bicycle and be in the heart of another culture overnight.

One summer, for example, our American Jesuit took his "push-bike," rode down to Southampton, had a turn about New Forest looking in vain for William Rufus, sailed past the Isle of Wight haunted by Tennyson and Victoria (you remember how she drove to his cottage one Sunday afternoon to complain about the moral tone of *Enoch Arden?*), and down the Solent into the roughest night he had ever spent at sea. From St. Malo he was able to ride along the coast of Brittany and join a Pardon at Plugastel, spend a breathless weekend racing the tides at Mont St. Michel, and see the tapestries at Caen before settling down in Paris for the Cours d'Eté at the Sorbonne. Like social climbers from various parts of France, he decided to have his accent lifted and was referred to a former star (strictly Third Empire) of the Comédie Française whose studio was on the top floor of a Left Bank apartment house. Here he found out among many other things that he had been making outrageous remarks all his life without any idea of their implications. Accent makes such a difference! The old lady was in gales of laughter much too often. But a summer in the Latin Quarter gave French literature a flavor that would have been hard to find sailing around Manhattan Island in July or even eating at the Canari d'Or on East 61st Street.

Italy was just as easy to reach and just as rewarding. In 1928 it was only six years after the Black Shirts had marched on Rome—long before the fatal Axis had been formed—and one was able to study Fascism at first hand. There was a new university in Perugia set up by the government exclusively for foreigners, the *Regia Università Italiana per Stranieri da Perugia* with headquarters in the 18th century Palazzo Galenga just outside the old Etruscan Gate. It could boast of distinguished professors drawn from a dozen ancient seats of learning and assigned there especially by the Duce to impress the visitors with the glory of Italy. The lectures that year were all on the 17th century—a Baroque century not too familiar to our generation. They covered its history, its economics, its art, its music, its letters—but running through them all like a black wool thread was the unmistakable inference that Italianità to be glorious must be controlled—government controlled. That year the future of Italy was far from determined. All that was needed to preserve the obvious material gains she had made, and her freedom as well, was a system of independent higher education. Instead she had a string of government-supported, government-controlled, government-enslaved universities. The experience of that summer always made one American educator a little wary on the subject of federal aid to American schools, but he was grateful to Italy for a rich experience.

Perugia had amazing variety for a small city. It was like a dozen picturesque villages all put together on top of a hill. Siena was only a bus ride away, and Orvieto, and Gubbio (the wolf was dead). From one's window in the *pensione* he had a perfect view of Assisi on the opposite hill, with Porziuncula down in the valley below. That *pensione* incidentally was an important part of the summer course. Signora Moglie had nine other boarders, all of them interesting, eight mature students and one nice young Facist official who corrected their accents by mocking them. Each meal began in silence and ended hours later in a torrent of argument. Meanwhile the visiting Jesuit could assist in the old duomo with a regular parish Mass

and help the good Cappuccino who preached the
Mission on a stage in the middle of the nave. When
the summer was over he got back to Cambridge feeling like an authentic 17th century Italian—an experience which almost any student in the university
might duplicate at will.

Thus England could preserve in the middle '20s a
liberal arts tradition which had begun to fail in America a full two generations before. To the Cantab it was
not a mere course of studies, it was a way of life that
helped to explain why even Sir J. J. Thompson or
Baron Anatol von Hügel were arts men before they
were scientists. Of course it flourished more vigorously in Oxford and Cambridge than in London or
Birmingham where the inroads of modern conditions
were more obvious, but since the illusion was maintained with calm determination that no universities
existed outside of Oxford and Cambridge, the old
tradition was felt to be secure.

IV

In Hudson County

AFTER THE MEDIEVAL CEREMONY in the Senate House at Cambridge, the "homo" who had done his homage not only to the University but to the liberal arts, was now brimming over with enthusiasm at the prospect of having some small part in restoring their ancient dignity in America. He had convinced himself that his superiors would not have invested so many pounds, shillings and pence in his special studies if they had no intention of letting him follow his bent for teaching, and this conviction was confirmed by an appointment to give a graduate summer course at Fordham on 17th century English. Everything was progressing according to schedule and he was getting around to the very British Lord Herbert of Cherbury, when the President of the University informed him that while preparing his lectures on Massinger and Donne and Dorothy Osborne, he might also be quietly preparing himself for an educational nightmare. He told him that instead of teaching he was to be assigned in the fall to the Deanship of Fordham's Downtown Division. There were at that time five schools, graduate and undergraduate, a part-time faculty, limited facilities, thousands of students and one dean, all on a few floors of the Woolworth Building overlooking City Hall. It was the direct antithesis of everything that he had been dreaming about during the years of study in Europe which had just come to a close, but he resigned himself to a difficult situation, looked over the real estate, and met the faculty.

Suddenly, on August the fourteenth, word came that the signals had been changed. He was to report in Jersey City and take all steps necessary to bring Saint Peter's College back to life on September the twentieth. The old College had been a casualty of the First World War and the four little classrooms that it had occupied on Grand Street had long since been overrun by a large and vigorous high school.

So on August the sixteenth he arrived for his new

assignment, a stranger in a very strange land and as he walked past the secondhand clothing stores on lower Newark Avenue and threaded his way through the side streets over to the rectory, he could not but meditate grimly on the inscrutable ways of Divine Providence.

The local Father Rector had persuaded the local Bishop to petition the Father General of the Society of Jesus for the reopening of the College without anybody having too definite an idea of what was involved. Everyone seemed to think that he was doing someone else a favor. Father General thought that the Bishop was anxious to have Saint Peter's back on its feet and would probably make the necessary funds available through an organized appeal. His Excellency, on the other hand, thought that the Jesuits were anxious to reopen the College and would probably draw on their own "inexhaustible reserves." In any case, the rector assured the new dean that at the end of the year he would have a million dollars on hand for at least one new college building. His optimism was refreshing, but unfortunately groundless. Meanwhile they walked back to Newark Avenue, under a great pair of pants swinging over the sidewalk, and up to the fourth floor of the Chamber of Commerce Building. When they got off the elevator,

Father Rector said with enthusiasm and a touch of pride, "Here is your new College." "Where?" asked the dean. "Anywhere you want to put it." This was certainly an educator's ideal of a flexible unit! It was so flexible that there was not one book, one chair, or one piece of chalk to suggest its limits. The challenge was positively exhilarating, so they promptly picked out three offices for classrooms, with a fourth for administration, and then found a nice kitchen that would do admirably for a chemistry laboratory.

Late that afternoon, all by himself, the dean sat up on the roof of the rectory taking in the whole panorama from Boyle's Thirty Acres, still haunted by the spirit of Jack Dempsey, past the linoleum factory, down to Colgate's by the river. From the faint odor of hot fat that pervaded the neighborhood, he surmised that the perfume must be added to the soap in some other and more fortunate city. All in all it was worse than Downtown Fordham. How could anyone ever blueprint a college in conditions like these?

To make matters worse it was 1930. The deepest depression of modern times was in full swing, so that even if permission were to be granted to run a drive for a million dollars, no one had any money to give. What could the new college offer the public anyway? It had no campus, it had no buildings, it had no athletic reputation nor even facilities for acquiring one, it had no student union nor anything that promised the most ordinary social advantages. Suddenly the new dean realized that he was in full charge of an *idea exemplaris divina.* He was the dean of a college that was still in the Mind of God. And he laughed out loud all by himself on the roof.

But then he balanced this with the other side of the picture. He was not completely destitute. He had one intangible and two tangibles to work with. The intangible was the good-will which still existed everywhere toward the old Saint Peter's College buried in the tomb for 12 long years. That proved to be far beyond anything he had realized and in the six years to come, six of the most stimulating and delightful years of his life, he was to grow in esteem for the great teachers of the past who had created an atmosphere of such profound respect all over northern New Jersey. The graduates of the old College, which had offered nothing but the humanities, were in positions of honor and trust, known for their integrity, their reasoning power, and particularly for their eloquence. Such was the intangible. The first of the tangibles strangely enough was the location in lower Jersey City. Aesthetically it may have left something to be desired. It looked less like Cambridge than any place in the world, but it was at least a transportation center for students living in all parts of the metropolitan area. So for his first catalogue, the dean had a map drawn which showed One Newark Avenue as the center of the universe, and put Fordham University on a distant periphery near Bangor, Maine.

The location then was a valuable asset, but it was on the basis of the second tangible that the blueprint of the new College was drawn up. This asset consisted of a staff of six Jesuits which came to be known in the local press, after a suggestion from the dean's office, as Saint Peter's "Million-Dollar Faculty." One was a first-class chemist, who was a splendid teacher with very high scholastic ideals. One was a first-class mathematician, with an enthusiasm for debate which was to capitalize on the reputation of the ancient orators who had gone before and develop some of the best speakers in the State. One was a first-class humanist, a man of culture and intellect and divine impatience. He would have given Albert Einstein eighty-five for science and the thirty-five he deserved for philosophy and theology. The scholastics were two of the most talented in their year, unspoiled by contact with ordinary classes and ready to take on the best students we could get for them. The sixth was the dean, young and inexperienced and not too intelligent; the sort of man with a strong back and a head full of convictions who enjoyed coming down every morning in a brand new school and saying, "The tradition around here has always been. . . ."

There were no bad habits to overcome, no intrenched interests, no tired, disillusioned teachers, no students organized to passive resistance. So then and there it was determined, sitting on the roof looking at the linoleum factory, and in full smell of Colgate's down the street, that the new Saint Peter's College would be a novelty in American education. It would offer a first-class liberal arts course and teach only intelligent and ambitious students. In other words, it would give what it ought to give only to those who ought to get it—an almost unheard-of procedure. That meant that the dean would announce on the very opening day that Saint Peter's was not interested in numbers or in display. It had no interest in athletic or social prestige. When the question was asked on every hand: "When will you field a football team?" the answer was, "Never." When asked how many thousand students he hoped to have eventually, the answer was, "A maximum of six hundred." Thus, thirty years ago, the little College in the slums acted on a question which is still making headlines in the papers of today: "Who *should* go to college?"

Once the new dean had accepted the location in the abstract, it was not long before he realized that the crowded city was just the place for a shrine to the liberal arts. He could not deny that remote cloisters in the green hills have a certain charm and our nostalgia for them in after years can be tender. If he had had his undergraduate days to live again he would probably have weakened and looked for a cloister away from it all. But no matter what his own weakness might be, he would henceforth encourage a young man about to enter college to choose a small conservative institution in the metropolitan area of a great city, where he could keep a good grip on the past, live in the present and plan for the future. His favorite sales talk was beginning to take form.

"Such colleges," he convinced himself, "are strong because they never have to worry about registration, and unless they plunge recklessly and get into heavy debt, never have to lower their standards. Like all the rest they are begging for bequests and endowments, but most of them have all the tuition they can handle, and tuition goes a whole lot further than presidents with their tear-drenched faces are ever ready to admit in public. Another source of strength is their close and constant contact with today."

As he worked it out, it sounded very up to date

and yet it was just what his father would have said in 1540. A couple of old Latin hexameters used to describe the difference between Ignatius Loyola, and the other founders of great religious orders:

"Valles Bernardus, Benedictus colles amavit,
Oppida Franciscus, magnas, Ignatius, urbes."

The others loved the valleys, the hills and the little towns, but Ignatius loved the great big cities! And so did the young dean in time. From his windows in the Chamber of Commerce it was hard to spot the Groves of Academe beyond the chimneys and the masts of ships. No breath came to him of the wild thyme on Mt. Hymettus. He could not quite glimpse the depths of Homer's wine-colored sea. He could not hear the thousand laughing waves of Aeschylus above the roar of traffic. In short, the Cyclades were very far from Newark Avenue, but the liberal arts were right at home.

Only two baccalaureate degrees were to be conferred by the new college. The B.S.I was to be the reward of a stiff science course with plenty of literature, history and philosophy along the way. It provided for pre-meds and majors in physics, chemistry and biology. The A.B. was to be granted only to those who could translate their own diplomas. For the first six years, the proportion remained constant. Half the student body was in science, half in arts, and of the latter all took advanced Latin and about half of them, advanced Greek.

Those who preferred the B.S.II with a major in educational measurements or business administration had a half dozen other colleges in the Metropolitan area to choose from. Saint Peter's did not despise such courses but it was thinking of what Saint Augustine says in the *De Ordine:* "A young person who neglects the liberal arts may be pious and pure, but so long as he is to live as a man among men, I do not see how anyone can call him happy." He was mindful too of the guiding principle of Ignatius: there are many goods but time is short, concentrate on the greater good. Admitting that the liberal arts can be studied without reading the classics in the original, the new college was confident that it would be most successful in following its own 400-year-old tradition, a tradition that regarded a study of Latin and Greek literature and philosophy in the old language in which they were composed, as a most reliable approach to culture.

As it happened, this determination to sacrifice numbers in the pursuit of an ideal proved to be just the bait that was needed for the right sort of student. The

reputation acquired almost immediately for consist-
ent elimination of the unwilling and the unfit made
screening a simple process because the wrong type
went elsewhere automatically. The little faculty had
been counselled by some to "get the College first and
the standards later," but they were convinced that if
they started that way it would take too many years to
live down their past. They knew that in a great metropolis there are many publics. If the aim of a college
is size, and its public relations are identified with
big-time athletics, a certain class of candidates will
be attracted. But there are other classes to be considered too, and where the policy is selective and the
emphasis intellectual, a surprisingly large minority
group will respond notwithstanding the sacrifice of
a few collegiate flourishes.

Even if the picture had not been so bright from
this particular angle, it seemed to the dean (an in-
curable idealist) that from the point of view of an
apostle the Church needed, in addition to com-
petent middle-class institutions with something for
everybody, a few top-flight intellectual centers just to
prove that revelation and tradition can thrive in an
atmosphere of real learning. The good old Protestant
impression in America that the Catholic hierarchy
can crowd the churches and hold on to the faithful

only as long as they keep them in ignorance is still too widespread to be overlooked. There is of course even today an enormous amount of ignorance in the Church (a fair proportion of the enormous amount of ignorance in the United States) and the Church has to handle the simple with simplicity. Then there is a second group rapidly increasing in size and influence which includes many lay and ecclesiastical leaders, priests and religious, business and professional men and women, who need to know the reason for the Faith that is in them, through adequate and adult courses. Intelligent and energetic but not of a scholarly bent, they have a recognized capacity which is scaled to the average American college and are to a great extent already provided for.

In addition to this solid and dependable body, however, we need superior and enquiring minds which can keep on exploring truth for a lifetime and, like the great Pasteur, come closer every day to the Faith of a Breton peasant's wife. We have a complement of such minds now, but unless they are clerics or candidates for a high political office it is rare that outsiders are conscious of their religious convictions, so that the impression persists that American Catholics still specialize in hewing wood and drawing water. What the neighbors can more readily appraise is the standing of our educational institutions and that is an added reason for cultivating the Apostolate of Excellence. One strictly first-class college is enough to refute a sweeping generalization and why could not Saint Peter's, with its fresh start, be that sort of college? For a wonder the faculty was given a free hand and, although there was very little money in sight, no crippling compromises were ever demanded by Superiors.

Only once did the subject of income cloud the sky. It was during the second year when standards of admission and dismissal were so well maintained that the treasurer's office complained, and the young dean was cautioned by a gifted young rector recently appointed not to overplay his hand. Since the financial aspect of excellence was the only difficulty stressed, he offered to get money elsewhere if the plans for Saint Peter's were left undisturbed. The rector was agreeable, and the following September the Hudson College of Commerce and Finance enrolled its first students. They found in it a good utility institution on a level with the downtown schools of surrounding universities, where satisfactory courses were available to practically anyone with the ordinary high school pre-requisites and the price of admission. It was to be an evening program, for an unlimited number of part-time and full-time students, arranged on a credit basis, and leading to the degree of B.S. in Bus. Adm. Provision was made for the development of extension courses in other centers, where eventually a curriculum in education and perhaps other fields could be established. Hudson College would have its own seal, its school colors, teams and student organizations, but the superfluous profits would enable Saint Peter's to develop into a small high-class liberal arts college where a traditional Jesuit education could always be found.

Beginning work on the sixteenth of August, it was possible to open the doors a month later with 70 freshmen. At the end of the first quarter, 14 of them were dropped. It was not as cold-blooded as it sounds because the dean was planning a February class where the promising ones who had misjudged the situation could have a second chance, but the news spread fast and the students who survived learned what was expected of them.

What the dean himself learned over the next six years was that educators in general do not realize the potentiality for work that exists in every pleasure-loving American boy with brains enough to deserve a college education. He may groan and weep and exercise ingenuity worthy of a better cause to avoid exerting himself. But if from the start he knows that the faculty means business and if the pressure is turned on a little at a time without ever being re-laxed again, he ends up by taking twice as much edu-cation (nobody can *give* him an education!) as one would expect in the average institution. Or he trans-fers to more congenial surroundings which is a splen-did idea.

And so it happened at Saint Peter's. Real students came eventually from a radius of 50 miles precisely because they heard that there was a premium on hard work and brains, or because they wanted to study under a particular professor, or because it was said that top-flight medical schools would welcome any pre-med recommended by the little college on Newark Avenue.

At the earliest possible moment and before the first graduation, application was made for recognition by the regional accrediting body, though some thought it a hopeless gesture. The examiner sent was old Dr. Wilson Farrand, the scholarly son of a scholarly father, who had lived a long life in the glow of the liberal arts. Arriving from Princeton early in the morning and picking his way through the destitute neighborhood of Mayor Hague's grim City Hall, he began by assuring the dean that he could not hold out the faintest hope of recognition but that he had made the trip because he liked the tone of the letter which had been written to the Middle States Association. He had evidently absorbed the same impression at Princeton which the dean had absorbed on the banks of the Cam. He thought that the liberal arts could flourish only where the student could live a liberal arts way of life, in an atmosphere friendly to culture. He underestimated the old adage that the right college is a matter of the right student and the right teacher. Even a log in a forest is not necessary; sometimes a curbstone will do. Instead of leaving before lunch, as he had planned, Dr. Farrand remained until five in the afternoon. In parting with the little faculty, he let them know that his recommendation to the committee would be enthusiastic.

What impressed him most was not the new equipment, or the correctness of office procedure, or the degree to which the catalogue conformed to American standards, but the fact that Saint Peter's was conservative in the old sense of the word *conservare*. It was not only keeping up with the developments in the world of education as far as they were worth keeping up with, but gathering up and preserving the treasures that we had inherited from our fathers. It was making more sure than ever of the great essentials. It was watching each move made by the leaders of thought to see if it would lead them up or down.

As the old scholar talked with the young enthusiast late that afternoon, they agreed that America needed the past and needed it terribly. They realized that any civilization is 90% heirlooms and lessons and memories. Jacques Maritain had remarked a short time before: "We have killed our past and lost its sense of values. We have destroyed our confidence in authority and have gained no confidence in ourselves." That very Spring the dean had visited Abraham Flexner for a little shop talk over in New York and had listened to the same analysis of the situation from one of the wisest men of his generation. American higher education, according to Dr. Flexner, had fallen into a meaningless flux because the colleges of liberal arts had lost their sense of values. They had broken continuity with the past and, as a result, everybody from the Graduate School to the Pre-School Nursery was trying something new every day and this confusion—this motion without direction—was taken for progress. Under the circumstances the situation was not surprising. Today's theory had to be discarded on the morrow, because the only real reason for adopting it had been that it was not yesterday's.

Meanwhile Newton's Third Law was in quiet operation, and the reaction provoked by the scorn of tradition in America appeared in a burst of neo-humanism. This had been quietly building up since the turn of the century with books appearing sporadically that could be described as humanistic in sympathy, but the country awoke to its presence only about 1930 when a professor in his early forties named Norman Foerster edited *Humanism and America, Essays in the Outlook of American Civilization.* This publication sparked a picturesque debate that raged through the following decade and materially helped our young dean in winning a public for Saint Peter's.

It was easier for a Jesuit College in 1930 to support neo-humanism than it had been for Ignatius Loyola to champion the humanism of the 16th century, whose background had been revolution against the established order. The mood of renaissance humanism was one of impatience with the undisputed primacy of the philosophy and theology which had dominated the schools of Europe for centuries. The emphasis at that time was shifted from the heavenly city to the earthly city of man. With notable exceptions like St. Thomas More, the great humanists tended to make the classics an end in themselves, so that the founder

[94]

of the Society of Jesus might have been consistently unsympathetic with the new trend. After all he was not a classicist himself, nor a stylist, and he was not regarded as a scholar; but as an analyst he had few equals in his time. He knew that eternal principles have to be eternally adapted and that adaptation always involves analysis. Of course it was conceded that no matter what new fashions might come in with changing tastes, the primacy of the cultivated mind must be maintained over knowledge as such, but once assured on that point new fashions deserved analysis at least.

A key to his thinking can be studied in the famous letter on the humanities written by Father John Polanco, his secretary, to Father James Laynez who was in Bologna working at the Council of Trent (1547).

Father François De Dainville speaks of the letter as "a veritable lawyer's defense of the humanities" and goes on to say: "Paradoxical as it may seem at first glance, Ignatius in his quest for a happy medium (between the medieval and renaissance extremes) revealed himself as more profoundly humanist than were those who arrogated this title to themselves. It was to this Ignatian virtue of prudence (in the Latin meaning of the word), which was respectful of moderate progress and which did not violate the rhythm of human evolution, that his pedagogical work owes its deep humane value and enabled him, despite inevitable vicissitudes, to outlive Renaissance humanism." (*Les Jesuites et l'humanisme.*)

The neo-humanism of 1930 was thus in the general direction of Christian humanism because it had been evoked by opposition not, as in the 16th Century, to a tired and somewhat discredited scholasticism or what they called "the darkness and theologism of the Middle Ages," but to an influence that Saint Peter's was fighting too. This was a very vigorous and hostile philosophy emanating from the Teachers College of Columbia University and spreading rapidly across the country—the philosophy of scientism. This philosophy took it for granted that man had been successfully reduced to passions and emotions, and that these, like nature itself, belonged entirely in the realm of science. These neo-humanist allies were not exactly Christian humanists. They did not share the conviction that there is more happiness in having an intelligence illuminated by both faith and knowledge than one illuminated by knowledge alone, but The Dean in Jersey City loved them for their enemies and cheered them on.

One group that was tilting with them fiercely professed to be the most genuine humanists of the lot.

It called itself the American Humanist Association and included an assortment of scientists, philosophers and liberal ministers who seemed to regard the birthday of John Dewey as the symbol of a new age that would achieve a glorious blend of naturalism, scientism, methodicism, relativism, psychologism, scepticism and of course pelagianism. From the heat engendered, sparks fell on the man in the street. Humanism for a while was almost a religion. For example the probated will of an enthusiast who died in this decade reads: "I, William Floyd of 114 East 31st Street, New York City, believing in the Lord God Jehovah, being of sound mind and a humanist, do hereby publish and declare, etc." The pace was increasing and during the next six years interested observers would see humanism move from the ivory towers of the intellectuals to the dimly lighted caverns of international statesmen, but for the moment the war was being fought on paper.

At the center of every educational storm in those uncertain days was the original and energetic young president of the University of Chicago, Robert Maynard Hutchins. He was known among his adversaries on Morningside Heights as Thomas Aquinas Hutchins, because of his alleged weakness for the Schools of the Scholastics. He was not a scholastic really, but

[97]

like Foerster he was revolted at the barren and ruthless scientism of the current educational trend and was always saying things that fitted perfectly into Saint Peter's campaign to convince the people of New Jersey that they needed Christian humanism.

The general direction of the dean's argument appeared at the first meeting with the surviving alumni of the old college in the Spring of 1931. He told them that for all their lavish expenditure, the American colleges had been losing ground for years and remarked that only the day before the papers were featuring two pieces of bad news. One, that the Communists were out of hand in Spain; the other, that the levellers had pulled Yale off her pedestal and that henceforth lectures in civilization would be substituted there for Latin and Greek. He admitted that Latin and Greek were just as difficult as ever and that the results, though very real, were just as intangible as ever. "It is more than probable," he said, "that if we passed around the Ciceros tonight and asked the waiters to keep a sharp eye out for interlinears, even the old stars would fail us. But that is quite normal. No one expects you to be able to translate Latin and Greek all your life. But though you may have forgotten your classics years ago, your classics are still working for you in and after business hours." When

Dean Hawks heard of Yale's surrender, he remarked with a touch of pride: "Of course, such progress is inevitable. Columbia dropped the classics from the arts course twenty-five years ago," and he did not seem to realize that an obvious retort could be made. The dean suggested that perhaps he had not read the current issue of the *Atlantic Monthly* where a distinguished English visitor was quoted as noting that all the really educated people in America were over fifty —had graduated, that is to say, before Columbia and many like her had dropped the classics and the old ideals of teaching. For now there was very little real teaching being done anywhere. All the professors were too busy writing books on "Why boys are not learning anything." Though not comparable in style, the wave-length of the dean's address was the wavelength of the Chicago medievalists.

Inevitably the outspoken admiration of Robert Hutchins for the great thinkers of the 13th Century and his enthusiasm for Latin and Greek as an approach to modern culture led Catholic colleges to regard him as a natural ally. This, however, was always a source of annoyance to him. He did not like the implication that Chicago was following any established pattern whatever and was not enthusiastic about such institutions anyway. This he made embarrassingly clear at a dinner of the National Catholic Educational Association in the Windy City, when the committee was unwise enough to have him as the principal speaker. But whether he liked it or not, he was talking their language most of the time. This was even more true of Mortimer Adler, the brilliant scholastic philosopher from Columbia who joined him the year after he went to the middle west from Yale. Dr. Adler was a recognized authority on St. Augustine and a member of the National Catholic Philosophical Association and the Thomistic Institute, so that before long the wits of the Faculty Club were calling him "the Jew who is making Catholics out of Protestants." The Third Musketeer was Stringfellow Barr who had picked up a lot of sympathetic ideas in Oxford and Paris and Ghent which qualified him as Visiting Professor of Liberal Arts in a Hutchins University.

Together these three developed the "Great Books Program" which attracted so much attention in the 1930's. Fundamentally it was healthy, with a tap-root deep in the past—the old principle that the best education consists in first-hand contact with first-class minds; that learning about books is a poor substitute for reading them. These were truisms which no one could dispute. Harvard had already publicized the idea in selling its six-foot shelf of translated classics through which culture could be absorbed even by a Yale man at the expense of only fifteen minutes a day, while at Columbia College in the '20s Professor John Erskine had established an honors course based on the Great Books in translation. Where the Chicago medievalists reached debatable ground was in the selection of the books and in the arrangement of the undergraduate curriculum.

As the course was eventually launched in St. John's College, Annapolis, the chosen masterpieces were grouped in four languages—Greek, Latin, French and German—with each group confined to a single year. Thus Freshman was spent on Greek history and literature. In his little office overlooking Newark Avenue an ambitious dean had followed every step in the announced preparations and concluded that the system could fully succeed only with picked graduates of European secondary schools. If the ordinary run-of-the-mill American boy even from the first third of his high school class had to walk into Freshman and face the philosophy of Plato and Aristotle in the original without a good foundation in both Greek and metaphysics, he would be in a fog until Easter. Ideally, of course, the culture of Athens should be studied first, then Roman culture and later Modern European, but it seemed to a sympathetic outsider that the average maturity and preparation of the candidates would suggest the necessity of inverting the order and of relying more heavily on translations. Serving some years later with the President of St. John's on an Advisory Board of the C.B.S., the Jesuit was able to confirm his first impressions but always rejoiced that the courageous experiment had been made. Its effect on other colleges was stimulating. Even where there was no desire to imitate the full program, it played a part in the re-examination that resulted in the new faculty recommendations of the 1940's, and meanwhile gave the dean on Newark Avenue fresh grist for his mill.

For all its idealism however, St. Peter's had to acknowledge in a whisper that the liberal arts were at an unfair disadvantage in an office building situated in the slums. So within a year the search began for a campus that could be bought for a few obols and a couple of denarii. Dollars were out of the question. After a few false starts (the incorrigible dean with all his talk about how Ignatius loved the cities, was trying to get out into the green hills of Bergen County!) a small estate on the Hudson Boulevard was purchased where the first commencement was held under the open sky. Eighty Universities and Colleges were big enough to send their representatives that day with heartwarming messages of fellowship. The little college had arrived. The dean had a lump in his throat.

Some thought that a sour note had been struck on the Acropolis when the first building erected was not a Parthenon but a gymnasium. There were a few snide remarks about still another "stadium with a few classrooms attached." But the decision had been a wise one. The perfect teacher may be able to charm a class in the marketplace but the best coach in the world cannot get far with a basketball program unless he has a suitable floor to play on, and with all its devotion to learning the new college had never minimized the importance of physical training. Besides, the gymnasium was also a theatre, a ballroom, and a chapel.

Before long, just by putting one card party on top of another, two more buildings were added to the gymnasium and preparations set on foot to take possession during the summer months. At this juncture, when the tired dean felt like Moses in sight of the Promised Land, he was ordered to a new post. Six years of promoting this small college had convinced even himself that the boys in St. Peter's were fortunate in not being smothered by a huge student body, 75 acres of elaborate architecture, and a football team of national proportions. Now that he was to return to Fordham as President and rediscover the advantages of size, he recalled with some uneasiness the old story of the chameleon who turned red on red and green on green but finally exploded trying to make good on Scotch plaid.

V

In the Bronx

THE SCOTCH PLAID proved to be an exaggerated image, but there was a certain amount of adjustment involved. Fordham and St. Peter's had the same general purposes and both were Jesuit institutions, but Fordham had been subjected to many influences that St. Peter's had thus far escaped. For example, it was said at the time to be the largest Catholic University in the world and all the deans joined the treasurer in transports of joy at every additional hundred names that were added to the register. The former dean of St. Peter's reflected on the fact that his new responsibility was already as big as Oxford

and Cambridge put together and wondered what conclusion could be drawn. Surely the hours he intended
to spend in the offices of the various registrars would
reassure him.

Then there was the *regnum in regno,* with headquarters in the gymnasium, and a budget of $335,000
a year. For ten years the football team had been
building up to a position of pre-eminence that made
the Ram a symbol familiar in every American home.
The possibility of martyrdom could not be excluded,
but the new president knew that for his own peace of
soul he would have to check before long on some of
the more colorful gossip that had reached him in the
last six years from sources which he felt sure were
prejudiced. The check began somewhat sooner than
expected.

On his very first morning on the campus, passing
the gym in something of a fog, he was spied by the
custodian, Mr. Patrick Kenealy, who rushed down the
long flight of steps with both arms extended in welcome. Such enthusiasm was a little beyond the neces-
sities of the occasion, and sprang apparently from
discussions which Pat had overheard following the
news of the recent appointment. It seemed that a few
airy comments made at various times in support of
St. Peter's athletic ideals had been analyzed at Ford-

ham with some alarm. Formalities over, the new president was asked to inspect the equipment department on the spot. So in a matter of seconds, room after room was unlocked, and trunk after trunk had the lid thrown back to disclose innumerable golden helmets gleaming in the June sun. "Each one of them cost $46.50, Father! There is a fortune invested here." And so it was with balloon-silk pants, jerseys, sweaters, parkas, shoes, socks, blankets and intricate sets of harness that would have saved the lives of Godfrey de Bouillon's Crusaders! The new president was properly impressed, promised Pat that he would not do anything rash, and said a prayer under his breath that the inventory of the library would be equally overwhelming.

Next there was this sordid business of the balance sheet. Surprisingly enough the University was still operating without a budget; was still true to the patriarchal habits of an earlier day. When a moral person is in his nineties and inclined to be conservative anyway, he feels a lingering bias toward the status quo and in Fordham's good old status quo there wasn't any need for a budget. Before General Pershing's War it was just a small institution, handling a modest income of one hundred thousand dollars or so. If anyone needed anything, he had only to go to the president like a child to his father and be refused. After the Armistice, however, there was rapid growth here as everywhere, and more money than had ever been seen before. In the fabulous twenties, receipts so far exceeded expenses that no one seemed to worry about future obligations and resources, still less about budgets. Attention was focused on the necessary building for ever greater expansion. The lucky administrators of those days were like our early American pioneers who always felt that thousands of miles of fertile land and lordly forest lay before them, so why bother replacing trees or rotating crops? Suddenly out of the blue came 1929 and money went underground. That should have produced a budget in 1931 but it took five years to realize that "this temporary depression following Mr. Smith's defeat" was a long lived phenomenon. At least that was the local explanation.

Conferences then day after day, not with the professors of the liberal arts but with a veteran treasurer of extraordinary singlemindedness and an omniscient bursar, revealed that the property was currently valued at $8,112,320.78 (the 78 cents was added out of sheer vanity by the accounting department); with a faculty of 651 and more than 8,000 students, the ordinary expenses of operation were nearly a million and a half a year with total expenditures of over three million. Moreover a debt of $340,000 had been incurred and all available resources spent on the university's most recent and most magnificent edifice, still four months from completion. At the end of the fiscal year, due in three days, there would be an operating deficit for the first time since the sinking of the *Lusitania*.

This was a shock, as the new president had already thought of several ornamental ways of spending money that would make Fordham a center of the liberal arts and a symbol of conservative culture. The sense of shock persisted and many an evening in the years to come he would walk around Edwards Parade by moonlight when the great pile of Tudor Gothic (with its $267,000 clock) looked as unsubstantial as a dream against the drifting clouds, and for some reason would always remember the Trojan elders above the Skean Gate watching Helen, the daughter of Zeus pass by. She was certainly all that Homer said she was and they were only human, but still they wished that she had never come to Troy.

Last of all there was that burgeoning faculty, 651 men and women, 53 of them members of the Society of Jesus. In quality they ranged like most faculties from eminent to inadequate, but were raised above average by a group ideal and a traditional method that was still recognizable. The only thing that made the new president uneasy was the unmistakable influence of old habits and vested interests of every sort. When he wanted to propose a change in scope or procedure, it was no longer possible to come down to his desk in the morning and say with a smile "The custom of this university has always been. . . ." Time and again in a great old-fashioned office big enough for Mussolini, he was to put his shoulder to one wheel after another only to realize that nothing was happening. This impressed him as a handicap peculiar to age and size, as well as the principal problem in his readjustment.

Outside the gate, much greater problems were taking shape though not yet recognized as Fordham's. The clouds of depression were lifting all too gradually. Ethiopia was finished, Hitler had marched into the Rhineland, France had ratified the Soviet agreement, and England was reeling under the impact of Mrs. Simpson. Europe had certainly reason enough to be nervous, and over here Roosevelt had just been renominated by acclamation. Most ominous of all, the dress rehearsal for World War II was opening in Spain. President Zamora had been deposed, churches, seminaries and convents burned by the Reds with

Soviet inspiration, and thousands of bishops, priests and religious slaughtered by the so-called Republicans, soon to be known through our liberal press as the Loyalists. The stage was already set. The assassination of Calvo Sotelo in the following month would be the signal for the Civil War.

A gift of prophecy that June would have warned the new president of Fordham that he had better prepare for three years of anxious neutrality, followed by two years of lend-lease and compulsory military service, leading up to the final crash. It was no time for educational planning, but happily not a prophet was in sight. What he wanted in general was first and foremost a college that was still unmistakably Jesuit, and that he found on his arrival. It was true that there were more students than could be handled efficiently, entrance requirements were too generous, and business administration was elbowing the arts and sciences in their own backyard, but at least the plague of pre-professional courses, so popular after the First World War, had vanished. Pre-medicine already involved an A.B. or a B.S.I, and even pre-law was beginning to mean four years of College. So that by transferring business administration to the School of Business, by maintaining the dominance of philosophy as the great coordinator, and by bolstering Latin and Greek with several forms of subtle kudos, it was still possible for faculty and students to hold their own in any discussion of the liberal arts.

The general framework was tightened by a well planned orientation course, introduced for the freshmen, which set all their work in perspective and showed the new men from hundreds of high schools how to analyze their hundreds of study problems. Of wider scope was the guidance program with a system of faculty interviews that began in Freshman and ended only with graduation. By way of compromise with Madison Avenue, there were special courses for Junior and a "man marketing clinic" that took 400 liberal arts and science men out of the groves of academe long enough to learn that they must not just look for a job but "merchandize a service." But in compensation the outlines of an Honors Course began to appear owing to the new policy of segregating the best brains for special attention and giving them all the extra work they could absorb. Of course it was a little confusing for an old Cantab who thought of Honors as the normal thing and a Pass Course as an accommodation for a slightly embarrassing minority, to find that in the planning that was being done 90% of the students were expected to be in the Pass Course. Eventually the select few who persevered in Honors were to be awarded their degrees not with praise or great praise or even highest praise (a bright pass man could get that) but with *Egregia cum laude* which might be freely translated "with hysterical praise." However, it was all in the right direction.

Comprehensive examinations and a dissertation in the major field introduced in 1938 proved an additional stimulus for the well-poised upper classmen, and contributed to the awakening interest in the liberal arts research which followed the transfer to the campus of the Graduate School with its "100 courses" open to upper classmen. It was consoling to know that twenty men in the class of 1939, who in an earlier day would have gone to the Law School *en masse*, elected instead the long road to the Ph.D.

Meanwhile two old-style Jesuit academies had been added to the extra-curricular program. One carried forward the tradition of the 1920 Playshop and kept the Little Theatre on the top floor of the Graduate School buzzing with original short pieces —every sort of thing from classical tragedies to musical comedies and even a surrealistic piece in ballet expression. There were full-length plays too. The most successful of these, *Who Ride on White Horses,* ran for a week on Broadway and was published afterwards. It is still produced by many amateur groups.

This constant fusing of experiment with tradition was further emphasized by a second academy devoted to the production of classics in the original. It began modestly enough with an English version of *Agamemnon* but soon moved on to a program that included, in one evening, scenes from *The Clouds* of Aristophanes in Greek, the *Aulularia* of Plautus in Latin and *Le Bourgeois Gentilhomme* of Molière in French. This was building up to the entire *Oedipus Rex* of Sophocles in Greek. On its last night the performance was given for the Greek War Relief and the audience, being almost exclusively Greek, whispered and murmured with excitement as each familiar scene unfolded, but on the first two nights no one seemed to breathe. Classical scholars were there from more than fifty different Colleges and Universities and their enthusiasm was extraordinary. William Reva had devised an impressive set with a great flight of steps and enormous columns, the lighting was designed by Jo Mielziner, while the music which had been written for the occasion by Virgil Thompson wrapped the action in appropriate gloom. Sophocles, as usual, did pretty well himself but it was the students who carried off the palm. Under the direction of Eric Hawkins the chorus triumphantly proved their necessity and the principals were beyond praise. Behind the whole thing was a human dynamo, a small and somewhat absentminded scholastic with a genius for getting things done right. The next year the *Eumenides* of Aeschylus was equally successful, and if times had been normal it would not have been difficult to interest one of the great foundations in making this important work a permanent tradition, but by then the war was breathing on our necks.

Long before there was any crisis, however, when most of us were still convinced that Europe could sink in the sea like another Atlantis without changing our way of life, a less glamorous matter than Greek drama had to be decided. It concerned the advantages of having resident students in a liberal arts college. For years Fordham had kept an open mind on the subject and did not increase its facilities. Of the nearly 1,620 college students registered in 1936, all but 120 went home every afternoon and 100 of those who remained were athletes with scholarships. The fact was that many members of the faculty had always been in favor of dropping the boarders altogether. From his experience as a scholastic prefecting the corridors, the president was convinced that the college needed more than New York boys could give

[117]

it. He was a New Yorker himself, born and bred, so that there was no small-town prejudice in this conviction, and he had seen the leadership displayed by New Yorkers when they moved out of the capital into "the provinces." But here in the Bronx, they displayed the same tendencies that were noticeable in Columbia and N.Y.U. They were capable enough but showed signs of narrowness, selfishness and pseudo-sophistication that could be modified only by a breeze from the great beyond and a fireplace on the campus. So first of all, plans were made at once to increase the proportion of boarders and eventually out of the 1,350 students who survived the new entrance requirements, 700 were living in. Next came the erection of two new residence halls, St. Robert's and Bishop's that were built around a panelled living room with an open fire. Finally, regional scholarships were established that brought each year a group of natural leaders from all the Jesuit high schools of the country. It did something for the local men-about-town to see boys from Oregon, Nebraska, and Louisiana taking the lead in class elections and bursting with enthusiasm for an alma mater which they themselves were inclined to take for granted.

As for the graduate and professional schools in 1936, it was considered enough if they ranked not

with the dazzling few whose endowments reached
hundreds of millions, but with that solid phalanx of
American institutions that keep abreast of the times
and offer their students more than they can actually
absorb.

It seemed a little late to open discussion on the
advisability of having such schools. There they were,
for better or worse. Some might envy the College of
the Holy Cross for its decision to concentrate on undergraduate training, but as far as Fordham was
concerned the die had been cast. In an earlier day
no one seemed to have considered any problem too
formidable for the next generation to solve, but it
was not entirely a policy of "After me, the deluge."
It was rather a race for prestige, coupled with zeal
for souls that had raised a whole crop of varied
faculties with varied problems across the country.
That and the cruel delusion that they would be a
source of additional revenue. They were—for a while.

By 1936, however, a dilemma presented itself:
either these schools would be high class and a financial drain on the undergraduate departments, or prof-
itably low class and a handicap for the alumni. The
young president with "the bright lexicon" under one
arm and stars in his eyes accepted the first horn. So between 1936 and 1938, with accumulating deficits,

accreditation was obtained, not without expenditure from the Association of American Universities, the Association of American Law Schools, the American Bar Association, the Association of Colleges of Pharmacy and the Association of Schools of Business. All this had been greatly facilitated by the excellent groundwork of a previous administration which had provided separate deans for each of the downtown schools, had increased the full time faculty, and set up something of a reference library that was a great improvement over the situation of 1930. But rented space always means limited space and the Woolworth Building had a connotation of the five-and-ten that was hard to forget. This was especially embarrassing for advanced research, so that while the ultimate transfer of the whole downtown division to Fordham's own university buildings was one of the earliest decisions made, priority was given to the needs of the graduate school.

The opportunity for a move presented itself in less than six months when the Tudor Gothic Dream was to be dedicated. His Eminence Patrick Cardinal Hayes who presided on that occasion could remember how difficult it was at one time to persuade Catholic parents that a high school education was a necessity. Later they were skeptical about wasting four years in college. But the colleges grew, professional schools flourished, and with the march of progress the demand had come for strictly graduate study. Some there were who regarded this further step as a useless luxury. In the beginning they used to say: "The boy has been to a parochial school, a public high school won't hurt him"; a few years later: "He has been to a Catholic high school, what difference can the college make?" and in 1936 we could still hear, in some quarters: "If he has prepared at a Catholic College, any graduate school will do." The last objector, like the first, overlooked the essential nature of Catholicism. For Catholicism is not to be found in any one book or course. It is a frame of mind, a point of view, an attitude toward the almost infinite number of tiny crises that arise in life. It is a culture of other-worldliness that flavors and illumines not only our conduct but our knowledge.

This the Holy Father had in mind when he insisted that if the culture of the non-sectarian universities is inimical to Catholic culture, Catholics must maintain their own schools even to the highest grade of university research at least in those departments essential to the defense of the Faith. Hence, the education program of the New York Archdiocese called for the graduate crown, and providing it was a proud duty and privilege. It was a privilege that meant happiness, and a duty that meant sacrifice. It was therefore a burden that pressed hard upon our shoulders, but there was plenty of joy in carrying it, because the future was so bright. We had at least a structure worthy of the work, not merely in point of facilities and equipment, but in the more intangible and important matter of inspiration. The building, however, was only the shell. Our hopes rested with the faculty and students. Year by year the standards rose as more and more distinguished men and women joined our staff of instruction and an ever greater proportion of full-time students came to work with them. To supplement the direction of our own professors with a different point of view, we planned to bring special lecturers from Europe who would remain for a whole semester as part of the Fordham faculty. We hoped to interest intellectual men of wealth in publications which were profitable in every way except financially. We planned to integrate the work of the college and graduate school so that an ever increasing number of Seniors would go on to graduate work.

It was sweet to dream, but wonderful to see the dream take on substantiality. It was sweet to spend money as if we had it, but wonderful to feel that we were the sort of reckless spendthrifts that Christ loved—that we were giving to the limit for Christian humanism, winning respect for the Catholic view of life, shaping intellectual leaders, living for the truth. And so although the picturesque details were lacking that day, the spirit was the spirit of the 13th century garret in the University of Paris. We had gone down to a city which was not medieval, but which had a few crooked lanes of its own and had sold, not a fur-lined cap or a jewelled dagger, but all our available securities, to buy not a ponderous vellum tome by Peter Lombard, but a Graduate School.

By the following September about half the graduate courses were being given on the campus; a year later the entire school was functioning in its new building. We had expected to lose a few hundred students by moving from the center of transportation to the outskirts of the city, and were reconciled to the sacrifice because of the cultural advantages we were sure to gain. Surprisingly enough the enrollment increased. It was even more encouraging to see the number of full-time students rise from 147 to 223. The registrants were evidently more concerned with adequate library facilities, consultation rooms, and an academic atmosphere than with the proximity of subways.

Within two weeks the president had a caller, Mrs.

Patrick McGovern, an old lady otherwise unknown to him. She told him with a delicate brogue that, having attended the dedication, she would like to help along the project for the building of a hostel where nuns could have congenial surroundings while taking their degrees. "I have the widow's mite here now if you want it," she added, and quietly wrote out a check that covered the entire cost of erecting and furnishing St. Mary's Hall, a residence for 50 nuns. When the president recovered consciousness he was not too sure about the vision, but the signature on his desk was genuine.

By the end of a year, the original anxieties had been resolved. The overcrowding could be kept in line by the higher standards adopted. The finances were far from hopeless. The annual deficit decreased, in spite of the fact that expenses were greater. The situation in the Athletic Association proved on examination to be above reproach at least according to American standards. The memory of any old afternoon in Cambridge made the whole thing look unbalanced, and no one could deny that the scale of operations created a false sense of values, but there was nothing crooked going on that would call for radical measures. So a much relieved young cleric enjoyed the autumn afternoons in his box on the 50-

yard line, and became in time an expert if not in calling the next play, at least in estimating the gate at a glance.

The faculty in the college resented at first the requirement that they have at least a Master's Degree (23 had only a Bachelor's) but when a generous salary scale was fixed, rank clarified and tenure granted, relations steadily improved. The student body while not homogeneous, contained a first class top third, and among the students in this group, the liberal arts were flourishing. The Virgilian Actus, oratorical contests, prize essays, excellent choral societies and so on, were all indicative that the breeze was blowing from the right direction.

On a memorable All Soul's Day in 1936 the then Eugenio Cardinal Pacelli had been received at the university. The air was electric. The five thousand people from the sidewalks of New York who waited on the Edwards Parade and the three thousand guests in the gymnasium were confident that he was not merely the Cardinal Secretary of State but the future Pope. After his election as Pius XII he wrote a treasured letter to Fordham in which he said:

"Speaking some years ago to the large gathering of friends and students who had assembled on the campus to welcome us to your university, we reminded you that your future is rich in promise because you cherish the priceless inheritance of the past; and in urging you to be true to the traditions, the principles, the ideals of Fordham, we assured you that in doing so, you would not only be serving God and Country, but that you would likewise be meriting for yourselves an incorruptible crown which should be yours for all eternity."

The president's preoccupation with this "priceless inheritance of the past" implied no blanket condemnation of the present. As Carlyle warned Emerson in 1842, "A man has no right to say to his own generation, turning quite away from it, 'Be damned.' It is the whole past and the whole present, this same cotton spinning, dollar hunting, canting and shrieking, very wretched generation of ours." But about the time of the Cardinal's visit, Walter de la Mare was writing: "The very years we now so actively occupy will soon be packed up in an old satchel labeled 'The 30's' and our little hot, cold, violent, affected, brand-new, exquisite, fresh little habits of mind, our manners, our hobbies, fashions, ideals, will have thinned and vanished away, will steadily have evaporated leaving only a frigid deposit of history; that is, a few decaying buildings, a few pictures, some music, some machine-made devices, and an immense quantity of print—most of it never to be disturbed again."

Had he written the lines in 1939 he would have included a few nightmares in the items to be packed. Looking back even on the restricted life of a university campus, one has to make an effort to remember that in the closing years of "The 30's" there were such consoling items as negotiations for *Thought*, a quarterly magazine destined for scholarly distinction, the reorganization of the Fordham University Press, a pavilion at the World's Fair devoted to the activities of the Seismological Observatory and visited by 800 people an hour. Yet these things were all real enough. There was also a Summer School Abroad, when a branch of the French department was transplanted to Grenoble. But intellectual things were beginning to seem unsubstantial. No one went so far as to say that thinking was fiddling, but everyone knew that Rome was starting to burn.

By 1938 history was rushing forward so tumultuously that it was hard to say what kind of European map the children would be studying when they returned to school in September. Fantastic things were happening. Anything gained credence. Men were speaking now of a Russian-German Alliance. It didn't make sense, but neither did the story of the previous five years. For example, the university had sent out invitations to discuss the need of federating the states in the Danube Valley. When the invitations were printed the average American was not aware that the Danube Valley was actually or potentially a danger spot. Even the governments concerned who should have known better regarded the proposition as debatable and almost academic. Austria was the first to accept. France and Poland followed. Germany was courteous but non-committal, while Italy sent assurances of full cooperation. In fact the whole thing was so interesting to official Washington that at least four ministers had expressed a desire to speak in person. But overnight, history was motorized and travelled a century in a single week. The national independence referendum proposed by the heroic von Schuschnigg was suddenly postponed until Hitler could arrive and cast the only ballot. Italy turned its back, France shrugged its shoulders, and England cried "O dear!" In 24 hours a nation died and was buried, so the committee at Fordham had to tear up its program and start all over again.

Conditions worsened as the year wore on. In November Father President joined Herbert Hoover in a radio protest against the persecution of Jews that had come to a head. He pointed out an influence at work in the Third Reich, mightier and more sinister than greed for either place or gold. What Cardinal Faulhaber and Cardinal Innitzer could see just then through broken panes of glass was the same influence that St. Jerome had seen through his tears when they told him that Rome was burning, the same influence that was sweeping over Northern Africa when Augustine turned his face to the wall and died. For Alaric had returned and Genseric and Attila the Hun —Attila who called himself the scourge of God, except that the first Attila had never been a Christian and had never partaken of the sacraments. The early Huns had always been barbarians. The fact that the National Socialists were born in a civilized fatherland, a glorious Germany rich in cultural traditions, dotted with churches whose lovely painted windows shone with German saints—this fact gave their campaign of frightfulness a very profound significance, a significance as profound as hell.

As 1939 wore on, the specter of our being drawn into the conflict would not down, in spite of a forced optimism which argued that since everyone would lose another World War, nobody wanted one. Speculation was the order of the day. It still seemed possible that this suicidal war might break and, if it did, two things might happen. Germany might collapse under the internal strain and the gallantry of the Poles—for the Poles were rated the best fighters in Europe. In that case, Russia and Italy would almost certainly stand aside, and the western powers would probably assemble again at another Versailles. Having, like the Bourbons, learned nothing and forgotten nothing, their one object might again be to dig a grave for Germany. If such a grave were begun a second time, it could well end up large enough to hold all Western Europe. On the other hand, however, Germany might succeed in crushing Poland on schedule. That would mean a long war, with Russian and Italian participation still very doubtful; but in the end, though it seemed impossible that Germany could win, her adversaries might very well bleed to death with her. Of course, even that, disastrous as it would be, would not mean the end of civilization. Still less would it be any reason for sending our boys to war. If Europe lost to North and South America the hegemony it had held since the age of Pericles, and became like Asia Minor and Northern Africa which once upon a time had their own day in the sun, it would mean a different world, but perhaps, who knows, a better one. Naturally we all dreaded the thought of such things because they meant the beginning of a new order, an altogether mysterious cycle of history, which was as hard for us to anticipate as modern times would have been for Charlemagne. But, even so, we felt very strongly that the politician who would risk the destruction of the United States of America in order to preserve the leadership of Europe, still more the leadership of any single European Empire, must be regarded as the dangerous enemy of his own country.

Then it began to look as if none of these dreadful things would happen for many years. Henry Ford had over-simplified the situation when he said that all the nations in Europe were merely bluffing, but it was obvious that nobody wanted a war and that in itself was momentous. It seemed to be a situation most unusual in European history and most encouraging. For if all the nations were equally appalled at the prospect of a general war, as they seemed to be, they were in the best possible mood for arriving at a just peace. Yet even as we were speculating, the German Panzers were rolling into Poland.

Early in September the delegates of Pax Romana held their first American Congress at Fordham. Two years previously they had asked the university to invite them to this country and thereupon had selected New York for their 1939 meeting. Later it was decided to hold the preliminary study sessions in Washington, but it was at a Pontifical Mass in St. Patrick's

Cathedral that the Pax Romana opened its Congress for the first time in the Western World. Delegates had come from all parts of Europe to meet their fellows from North and South America in a week of spiritual exercises and intellectual conferences. It is true that the Pax Romana had never been primarily a League of Peace. Only one speech planned for the Congress dealt with peace directly. But the ultimate object of all cooperation is peace, and the ultimate object of international student cooperation is international peace, the peace of Christ. So now their great day had come. They had met to further international understanding—and they could hardly hear themselves think, for the rattle of sabers and crash of guns. To a cynical modern there was a certain heartless humor in the situation. So many fine young people praying and talking and playing together with the one object that their relatives stop hating one another, and reading every day in the papers fresh evidence that European civilization was falling apart. "What good can they think they are doing? Why don't they give up and go back to whatever is left of home and get behind a machine gun like the rest? Physical strength is the only thing that matters anyway, and all nations are equally immoral." That was the way people were talking in the street. It was so

easy to be cynical and superficial—never easier, perhaps, than in 1939 when education was spread so
wide and so very thin; when international relations
were so confused by half-baked ideologies and the
common people so bewildered by propaganda. And
yet, though the cynics seemed to prevail, they were
just as stupid as they ever were. They were missing
the point as usual, The Divine Point at which all creation comes to focus. The members of the Pax Romana
were blessed with the unbounded optimism of youth.
With radiant smiles on their lips they cried, "The
future belongs to us," while we poor aging bewildered wrecks shook our heads and said, "You're
right, God help you!" Thus we finished, with a
troubled prayer, the packing of an old satchel labeled
"The '30s."

VI

In a Hot War

ON TOP OF A BOOKCASE in the president's office at Fordham there is a small bronze of some artistic value. It is evidently an antique and represents a very old man with a long square beard, vested in an elaborate cope that might have been designed by Cellini. The head is slightly bowed, the eyes are piercing, the brow has all the disillusioned repose of an aged diplomat. It is a contemporary likeness of the great Farnese Pope, Paul III, which came to Fordham in 1940 as the gift of an Italian nobleman to mark the four hundredth anniversary of the Jesuit Order. For it was in 1540, at the height of the glittering renaissance, that

[135]

His Holiness, Pope Paul III, recognized as a Religious Order a group of young scholars calling themselves The Company of Jesus, Societas Jesu, whose successors were to be known in history not always with equal enthusiasm, but never with indifference, as Jesuits. After 400 years of a very checkered career, a career which for bright light and black shadow had not been equalled in the history of the Church, The Society of Jesus all over the world was chanting a *Te Deum*, with a deep and spiritual joy difficult to interpret for outsiders especially in such doubtful times.

Over their celebration the shadows prevailed. In Europe, Asia, and Africa the immediate future of the Society trembled again in the balance as it had trembled so often before. Throughout Great Britain, where it had been unmolested for a hundred, happy and successful years, no one knew what the next sunrise would bring. The Continent was even darker.

Its American sons were living in the sunshine. Their seven Provinces, while harassed as usual by financial problems, were looking forward to ever greater opportunities for service. They did not feel that they were more abundantly blessed by God than their brothers in the wracked and torn parts of the world, for they knew that apostolic service is ennobled by suffering. Father President took his little bronze

Farnese down from the bookcase and made a place for him on a very disorderly desk. He wondered what a vision of these 400 years of Jesuit history might have done for his bent old head and general disillusionment. He wondered too what the next ten years might add to that history.

Just the day before, at the College Commencement, the officers of the ROTC had come up to receive their commissions as Second Lieutenants of the Reserve. For the moment, they had cast aside their academic gowns and stood in their military uniforms, proud, happy, chests out, grand boys. Nobody mentioned the war—parents are entitled to one night of happiness. But the resolution was already made to establish a Students' Army Training Corps, if the times should require it, and turn the campus into an armed camp as in 1917. But military preparedness, without moral preparedness, is always suicide. Far more important than drilling the boys in the use of a gun was the drilling that was necessary to keep them clear-headed on the fundamental principles of morality, the natural law, natural rights and duties, responsibility and freedom of the will, self-control, the necessity of a clean family life, authority and religion. In addition there was a little purely intellectual drilling that could not be neglected without courting disaster. For higher education is not a mere luxury to set aside in time of war. It is an absolute necessity if the higher life of a nation is to endure. A mighty army can always be raised without universities and colleges. In fact, the less liberal education a soldier has, the better instrument of fanaticism he becomes. But there will no longer be a nation—a moral union of families, cooperating for the good of all.

So, in spite of everything, Fordham went quietly ahead with its Centenary plans for 1941. It looked for substantial help from all who realized that ignorance, in the end, is worse than hunger or a broken leg; who realized that all patriotism is good, but that the most far-sighted patriotism is that which brings the greatest ultimate happiness, the patriotism which brings truth to a future generation.

This note was sounded again late in October when the Commander-in-Chief of the Army and Navy paid a ceremonial visit to the campus. His coming had been contrived. The big campaign was on and Wendell Willkie was offering more resistance than had been expected by the Democratic strategists. At the height of the struggle his manager called on the head of Fordham, a notorious third-generation Republican, and inquired about the possibility of an honorary degree. The Jesuit parried with the suggestion that both candidates might speak to the youth of the nation (coast to coast) from the terrace in front of the Graduate School. Mr. Willkie accepted at once, but word came from the White House that F.D.R. would on no condition share the platform with W.W. The next week Mr. Willkie wrote to the Athletic Association asking them to reserve tickets for him at the Fordham —St. Mary's game, and was naturally invited to share the official box. This caused considerable excitement among the predominantly Democratic alumni, until it was suggested that if Roosevelt should come to the campus he would be fittingly received. The next day the Democratic leader of the Bronx telephoned to say that a formal invitation if extended would be accepted. The occasion was a review of the R.O.T.C., and on October 28th a cavalcade of distinguished personalities, which included His Excellency the Archbishop and His Excellency the Governor, arrived with the President of the United States. As Willkie's visit was on Saturday and Roosevelt's on the following Monday, it was no wonder that the Freshmen were told by the Sophomores to expect the Communist Earl Browder for benediction on Sunday.

The host of the occasion, standing in the car beside a famous figure he had never fully appreciated, began his remarks by reminding the large crowd of

visitors and the students drawn up in military for-
mation, of their Commander-in-Chief's earliest associations with Fordham: "His father's cousin James
Roosevelt Bayley, built old St. John's and the Church
nearly a century ago, and last year his charming
mother (I still maintain, the most charming of all the
Roosevelts) came here in the pouring rain to unveil a
tablet erected in honor of Bishop Bayley. We were
all thoroughly drenched, and after the ceremony I
asked if she wouldn't like to step into my office to
warm up—with a glass of sherry. She replied: 'For
one awful moment I thought you were going to suggest a cup of tea.'. . . But I should perhaps point out
to the younger men who may not grasp the full significance of the present scene, that Mr. Roosevelt is
not just another President. In an era of unusually
dynamic personalities here and abroad he is without
doubt one of the three or four most dynamic. He will
be for our great grandchildren the symbol of our generation. Other Presidents have come and gone and
the quiet tide of American life has shown hardly a
ripple. How many of you students here could tell me
a single event that took place in the time of Chester
A. Arthur? Not one! Today you stand before a man
whose imprint is forever fixed on our national history.

Our country has been reshaped in the last eight years and will never again be just what it was before."

In reply the President who seemed to be much flattered, and threw his host a smile that was his to cherish forever, said how proud and happy he was as an old alumnus (LL.D. '29) to be back for the first time in a great many years: "I am glad to be here to see these members of the Battalion who know our National Preparedness Program. You know that we are to take this muster—and I like to call it muster because it is an old word that goes back to the old Colonial days in America when every able man had an obligation to serve his community and his country in case of attack." That word "muster" referring to the impending draft of young Americans seemed to give him great satisfaction. It was so much more disarming than "draft" or "compulsory Military Service" that it went out to the whole nation the next day in a milestone radio address.

The visit was over. Everyone cheered. The man who changed the face of America beamed on the crowd and waved. "My friends!" If he had stayed around another hour even a third generation Republican might have voted for him.

The next day saw the return to a normal uneasiness. Observers were already reporting that one of the most disastrous effects of the current war on civilians in Europe was the fact that nobody was planning for the future anymore. People tended to be absorbed in a mattress for the bombproof cellar, a drink of water, or a little more sugar "now." There might be no tomorrow.

Sometimes the president of Fordham had the same disturbing thought when a new blast of rumor came from the front. Somebody seemed to be whispering in the office, "Why prepare anything for next October? Stop your dreaming! Come down from your ivory tower and lend a hand to the Red Cross. The world has more serious things to consider now than books." Of course he knew the answer. Lives are lived for ideals, not for books, and he was not in an ivory tower. As he wrote to the Trustees in January of 1941: "We are manning a lighthouse, and the darker the clouds, the more need there is of light. We have our moments of weakness though, and doubt."

It all seemed such a pity. Just at the time when thoughtful educators were beginning to bring some order into American universities, and even the public was beginning to see the point; when life was returning to the teaching of the liberal arts and an appetite for something beyond facts was developing in American students, when hardheaded employers were be-

ginning to take an interest in the intangibles of a
cultured boy—along came a war and shifted all the
emphasis back to machines again. Just at the time
when Fordham was beginning to see its way clear to
the fulfillment of its dreams, a brilliant faculty and a
select student body with all the instruments they
needed for distinguished service, along came a war
and dried up the indispensable sources of help. A
survey of the seven largest cities of the United States
made about that time showed that gifts for education
were 30 per cent less than in 1939, and bequests had
been reduced by 40 per cent. Some former benefactors were engrossed in European relief, some were
worried about the expected rise of taxes, and some
were on the bread line.

But for the present, the faculty was going quietly
ahead as if events were comprehensible and the future secure. The fact was that they never felt more
necessary, and besides they had a centenary celebration on their hands. Just a hundred years before,
in the Fall of 1840, a young Irish American Bishop
named John Hughes was putting the finishing touches
on a new college up in Westchester. It was to be the
fulfillment of a dream. The struggling Catholics of
New York had realized for years that they could not
depend on Europe forever to supply the ranks of the

clergy, and so for the same reason that moved the Puritans of Boston to open Harvard University, they set about the foundation of a Catholic center of learning. It was to be the first in the East north of Maryland—the first, that is, which was destined to survive.

Actually the Jesuits had opened a school in Manhattan a century and a half before St. John's at Fordham was planned, for it was about 1683, under the patronage of Governor Thomas Dongan, that three Jesuits, Father Harvey, Father Harrison and Father Gage, began a Latin School near the site of the present Customs House at Bowling Green and many of the best people, Protestant and Catholic alike, sent their sons to be educated there. It had little competition in the old Dutch village and was doing rather well until William of Orange was put on the English throne by the big landowners of the Whig Party. Immediately penal laws of incredible barbarity were resurrected throughout the English possessions, which practically wiped out the Catholic colonists of New York and with them their precious little school. Had religious liberty survived the fall of James II, Fordham would be today one of the oldest universities in the United States. But religious liberty was crushed, and it was not until the British defeat in the Revolutionary War that a Catholic college was possible once more in the city of New York. So at length, after much planning and scraping of pennies, the New York Literary Institution was opened by Father Anthony Kohlmann, S. J. in 1809 on the site now occupied by St. Patrick's Cathedral, that is 'way out at 50th street about four miles from the city. Unfortunately, this venture was also abandoned after a few successful years, but not because of persecution, rather because of our own lack of foresight. The wise Father Kohlmann seemed to be the only one who realized that New York with its handful of Catholics had a future. His Southern superiors at Georgetown felt that the center of influence and development was destined to be in Washington, Baltimore and the counties of Maryland, where the old Catholic families had rich tobacco plantations, so why waste men on a sprawling seaport town? Had their forecast been more accurate, our second school at least would have survived and Fordham would have had a start of 23 years on New York University. As it was, when we finally opened our doors for good, N.Y.U. was a little place on Washington Square, just 9 years old, but Columbia was an old plutocrat of 87, well established on its first tract of land, down between Murray and Barclay Streets, already wickedly wealthy and determined even then never to take its football seriously.

[145]

The start we made, however, though delayed, was not too late to be picturesque. Our proud metropolis was still a quaint, old, provincial kind of place, nothing like gay and bustling Philadelphia (years were destined to pass before Jenny Lind and Charles Dickens would add the glamour of European capitals to our night life). Even so, there were signs of momentous change, momentous social and religious change. England, for one thing, had been forced to grant Catholic Emancipation in 1829; but the economic brutality which found its perfect expression in the famine of '47 continued to lash the unhappy Irish for another 30 years and drove them in hundreds of thousands to "a strange but happier land." That phrase from *The Wearing of the Green* tells better than anything else how ghastly their conditions were at home. For even in this happier land, instead of a welcome they found mobs of native-born hoodlums whose patriotism was expressed in the violence of bloodshed and arson. Here was a problem then for the young Catholic Bishop whose flock was expanding with incredible rapidity, who was conscious of bitter antagonism on every side especially in the privately controlled public schools, and who could rely on a very limited supply of priests. Here was a problem whose answer was to be the founding of Fordham University.

By the summer of 1841 all was in readiness, and on the feast day of his own patron, St. John the Baptist, the doors of the new institution were formally opened. As first President he appointed the Rev. Mr. John McClosky (priests were still called "Mr." in America in those days), a gentle and thoughtful man who was later to be the first Bishop of Albany, second Archbishop of New York and our first American Cardinal. Beginning with six students in the College and four in the Seminary, the Bishop's venture prospered from the very first day, and four years later was ready for a building program, the first in a series of which the end is not yet in sight.

To celebrate the Centenary, a special committee arranged a program of lectures and symposia that began the previous academic year with a three day philosophical discussion on American education. From September 1940, no month was without its appropriate observance until from September 15th to 17th, 1941, the celebration was concluded with fitting solemnity. The Holy Father, who wrote a beautiful letter for the occasion, was represented by His Excellency the Apostolic Delegate. The President of the United States sent Vice President Henry

C. Wallace in his stead. His Excellency the Archbishop of New York, the Governor of New York, the Lieutenant Governor, and the Secretary of State, the Mayor of the City of New York, 18 Most Reverend Archbishops and Bishops, and 92 College and University Presidents were among the throng of distinguished visitors who added prestige to the brilliant scholastic exercises that had been planned. One hundred and seventy-four scholars, well known in their irrespective fields, read and discussed original and important papers on everything from labor law to tectonophysics and Jordanus of Saxonia, but Latin, Greek, and philosophy had places of honor.

On the morning of the third day, the Centenary Convocation was held on the terrace of the Graduate School to welcome the delegates who had come from all over the United States, and from 18 foreign countries, to represent 446 Colleges and Universities and 125 Learned Societies.

In the midst of the celebration, however, no one could quite banish the formless fear that all this academic glory was a touch of autumn coloring, reminding us that another winter was at hand. Some more pessimistic observers called it rather another ice age that would end our particular cycle of civilization. No one tried to blame some individual tyrant for its approach. No one said, "There is only one enemy to destroy, one rattlesnake to scotch. If Democracy but attacks him now, with so many super-tanks and flying fortresses, vigor will return to our Christian principles. Our churches will be holy and our homes will be chaste again. There will be respect for marriage vows and love for children. Prosperity, hand in hand with social justice, will enter on the scene and educational institutions will return to educational pursuits." They knew that poor old Europe was already sick unto death long before she decided to end it all with an overdose of modernity. They knew that for years past our universities of Europe and America had been hacking away at the twin foundations of their own house. Like men gone mad with pride they had recklessly attacked Christianity and Hellenism as though they could by some legerdemain preserve Western Civilization and still destroy the two great traditions on which it rested. For years past wise men had been warning them that if they did not desist from their crazy undermining operations they would bring the roof down on all our heads. Now they had done it. Blame had to be placed exactly where it belonged. This annihilating war of ideas which was closing our hectic chapter of history came to us straight from the lecture halls of

Europe and America. It would have come sooner or later in any event.

Our brilliant professors who are long on information and short on wisdom would surely have found some other method of destroying us, if the tyrants of the modern world had happily died in their baptismal innocence. As it was our educators had prepared the way for intellectual slavery by giving us, in place of education, bewilderment. In place of wisdom, and at the expense of the sources of wisdom, they spread before their students more undigested information than the human race had ever had before; much more than the human race knew how to use. They had produced a glut of facts to which we at this time were not entitled, for no age is entitled to more facts than it has wisdom to assimilate.

Now that the harm was done, however, no one would declare a moratorium of information, but our universities had their work cut out for them: the gradual restoration of wisdom to the world. They were to push forward in every line of modern research with continued and breathless devotion, but like the athletes in the old Athenian torch race of Pan, they were never to run so fast that they put out the light. For the new world that we hoped would be born of all this pain must be "a brave new world," but not brave with the bravery of a dehumanized machine. We wanted no heroes of the Soviet type to shape our future for us; reckless heroes who were ready to throw away their lives in defense of indefensible principles which they never understood in the first place. We wanted the enlightened bravery of Christian humanism.

It would be an exaggeration to say that there was not a cloud in the sky, but none of the delegates could have realized that this was to be the last great academic pageant in the country before the upheaval. Many believed that public opinion would keep our boys on American soil—he had said it "again and again." Most believed that our resources were such that no one would dare attack us. But it was only a matter of a few short weeks before one air raid settled America's future role in world affairs. Of the 96 officers killed at Pearl Harbor, one was a Fordham boy of the class of '35, another of the class of '37.

On January 2nd the heads of all the colleges in the country were called together in Baltimore by Paul McNutt, to offer their resources to the government for the successful prosecution of the war. Some thought that they offered too much too soon, but they confidently expected to keep afloat until the storm was over. By the end of the year they knew that at least 50 of those who attended the meeting had been over optimistic, and all began to realize that if the war proved to be a long one 500 colleges might be sacrificed. As the hour arrived and each institution padlocked its memorial gates and boarded up the windows of its libraries and laboratories, faculty and students and alumni would say to a man: "If this has to be done to win the war, we are glad to make the sacrifice," but they would say it as they would speak about the sacrifice of their lives.

Even where the danger of closing was remote, the faculty had to cope with the eager pessimism of those who begrudged the smallest economy made for scholarship, the kind of people whose wish was father of the thought when they began in 1941 to cry that the liberal arts were done for. Aiding and abetting them was the superficial group that talked about being practical in our schools; who wanted to teach just democracy, tolerance and science, though unable to define any one of the three. Even at Fordham there were financial wizards to whom a university was just another grocery store: "If jello is not moving fast enough, you take it off the shelf. Why run a department or a school that does not pay?" And then the cynical sort with their genius for drying up all springs of inspiration: "Why pass out sheepskins to cannon-

fodder? You don't have to be a Doctor of Philosophy
to stop a bullet." Even intelligent and conscientious
students were being plagued by a sense of guilt in
studying Greek drama when empires were falling.
Finally, to round out the chorus of woe, there were
the Catholic enthusiasts promoting the idea that for
the glory of God and the good of the Church, all our
limited resources should be poured into more and
larger tea dances and discussion groups for Catholics
at non-Catholic Colleges. The struggle to maintain
our own intellectual and spiritual culture was "obviously impossible."

Resisting all these pressures, Fordham quietly
hoped to serve the country during the War in all the
usual ways that meet the eye but most of all in preserving for a better day the tranquillity of intellectual
order. It was a crucial year. The President of the University was holding his breath until he could see
what the Government would do to the colleges
through taxation and the lowering of the draft age,
but he resolved to take the advice of St. Ignatius
about making decisions in time of panic, and to meet
as far as humanly possible all financial obligations
without tearing apart the fabric of the university. He
realized that once an entire school has died, not many
men can say, *"Talitha cumi"* and have the maiden rise.

A sharp decline in registration during war years was to be expected. We were eventually to reach the point where the only men coming to lectures were under eighteen or classified as "4F." Had it not been for the 2,500 women students, the crisis in 1943 when the student body was cut in half would have been still more acute.

One target which the Imperial Japanese Air Force never knew they sank was the Fordham football squad. Soon after a triumphant return from the Sugar Bowl in New Orleans, the backfield and half the line left college to begin their flight training and the head coach joined the Navy about the same time, leaving one of his assistants to face an empty stadium in 1942. Another casualty of the war was the Centenary appeal for funds, which had already brought in about half of what had been expected before becoming hopelessly involved in Muzhaisk and the Burma Road.

Meanwhile an important experiment was being tried all over the country. Undergraduate courses had been reorganized so that the Bachelor's degree could be earned in three years. This acceleration was considered by most as a necessary evil following the draft, and was generally regarded by members of the faculty as a fraud. They pointed out that it pretended to do all that was done before, while ignoring the fact that it had eliminated the time necessary for study, reflection and growth. But some of the wisest of them admitted that much could be said for permanently reducing the matter required for a degree so that the course could be done in three years with adequate breaks allowed for.

Had this development taken place, it might have helped in solving the national problem of prolonged adolescence. This has been aggravated by the practice of forcing our youth to give half their lives to formal schooling on the assumption that they would never learn anything after graduation, instead of helping them to concentrate on the instruments with which they could make their whole lives an education. Twenty-two was accepted as a normal age for the earning of a Bachelor's degree. That meant finishing a graduate or professional school at twenty-six, postponing marriage until thirty. To be self-supporting at twenty-six, when for his own sake and the sake of society he should be the responsible head of a small family, a Bachelor's degree should be a possibility at eighteen. And it could be if, with wise economy, grammar school were reduced to six years, high school to three, and college to three.

Of course this presupposes a few changes which it

would be cynical to regard as unreasonable. First, a teacher should be able to teach and should have a clear idea of the objectives at various levels. Then the students, having been introduced early in life to real work, should be eliminated ruthlessly from training for which they have no capacity. Actually none of this came to pass, and acceleration went the way of rationing and blackouts. What surprised the president of Fordham was that it disappeared so quickly. He realized that, when the cease fire came along, there would be long-haired men and short-haired women who would want at once to tear down our national defenses, but he was convinced that the country would never disarm again. This conviction was the background of his address that opened the academic year of 1942.

"We have learned at last," he said to the student body assembled on the Edwards Parade, "that we can rely on no more barriers of time or place; that Isolationism is as dead as the A.P.A. Only a year ago there were loyal Americans, and I was one of them, who felt that this was not our war, that if we kept to ourselves, no one would dare to attack us. We used to say that if the Soviet were wiped off the face of the earth it would be good riddance and that the feeble and guilty old British Empire was not worth one

American life. We protested violently when we saw our president, as we used to put it, 'spoiling for a fight,' dragging us step by step into an endless and dreadful war which no enemy wanted to declare. Today it is humiliating, but many of us are ready to stand up in meeting and confess that we were wrong and he was right. It *was* our war from the first. If he had listened to us, China, Russia and Great Britain would now be prostrate and we should be facing our zero hour alone and unprepared. As it is, our strangely assorted allies are far from prostrate and their immense courage, backed up at last by the full power of the United States, will make this a long war with good news at the end.

"Of course, the longer the war, the longer the convalescence. Policing tasks that will face us for years to come will take as great an army as any offensive campaign, and cleaning up the wreckage, physical, financial and moral, at home and abroad, will require a large armed force for at least another generation. That is why I think acceleration is here to stay. We shall have to reserve a year out of our crowded young American lives for military service, and acceleration of the college program is the easiest if not the best way to provide for it."

The principal topic of his address was the adaptation of studies to world conditions, but the passage that attracted attention was the one that renounced isolationism and spoke about "our war." It was the occasion of 85 editorials in various parts of the country and was reported at length in the British press. In less than a month His Majesty's government suggested to Cardinal Hinsley that he invite the American Jesuit to give the Lenten Course in Westminster Cathedral. A million of his fellow countrymen were gathering in England preparatory to the invasion of the continent, and it was thought that they might like to hear their own mellifluous accent from the principal Catholic pulpit of London.

The sermons prepared in a hurry were the least interesting part of a trip that began with a bomber flight from Montreal to Prestwick in Scotland, from snow flurries to hawthorn hedges in bloom, and ended on a transport full of troops dodging submarines from the Firth of Forth to the Hudson River. All very hush hush! With headquarters at Farm Street, two blocks from the anti-aircraft guns in Hyde Park he spent three fascinating months travelling and lecturing around various parts of the Kingdom, but always getting back by Friday for the sermon at the Cathedral on Sunday evening after tea.

In London between air raids there was a steady

round of rationed luncheons, teas and dinners that resulted in the loss of thirty pounds in ninety days.
There were old friends, local clergy, exiled Poles,
American and Canadian chaplains, officers and en-
listed men and many interesting natives from every
walk of life. He spent the seventeenth of March for
example in Parliament; the morning with Brendan
Bracken in the House of Commons, where he happened on Winston Churchill in the corridor, lunch in
the Peers' dining room (Irish stew, by the way!) and
the afternoon with the Duke of Norfolk in the House
of Lords, convened in the King's robing-room. Out
of the 764 peers eligible for membership, 30 were
present that day, 27 more than required for the official
quorum. The visiting New Yorker was fortunate
enough to hear a spirited attack on Archbishop Spell-
man by Lord Wedgwood of the pottery family who
was promptly shattered by Lord Cranborne, the
Privy Seal. This scion of the Cecils, descended from
the Lord Burleigh who did in so many Jesuits in his
time, lounged on the rostrum in the best tradition of
the Oxford Union and began in a tired English voice:
"I have often listened to the Most Noble Lord without enthusiasm, but never have I heard him offend so
many people in so short a time." Congratulated after-

wards, he smiled and said: "Father, you must admit he was a sitting duck."

Later there was a luncheon given by His Majesty's Government, at which about 30 guests gathered to express the warmest sort of hospitality. A rationing that reduced the wealthy to essentials may have made it easy to collect celebrities at an unrationed government board even for a minor occasion, but the seating list was notable as showing thought and extraordinary courtesy. Conclusions could be drawn from it. This particular group formed a sampling of contemporary Britain that every visitor was not privileged to enjoy, but their friendliness was something that any American could meet with in the simplest pub. To a suspicious nature, it looked like a conspiracy of good will but it really sprang from a profound conviction everywhere that the destinies of the English-speaking world were joined. For all our differences we made up a group of decent people who shared Christianity and football and Wordsworth and collegiate Gothic and roast beef and the Bill of Rights. Having lived in England during the '20s when they owed us money which they had no intention of paying, and when the only social handicap worse than being an American was to be an Irish American Catholic, the visiting Jesuit was amazed to find that the average Englishman had softened toward the Catholic Church almost as much as he had toward the U.S.A.

For this Cardinal Hinsley was as much responsible as anyone. With the war as the occasion, he had brought about cooperation in many fields between Catholics, Anglicans and Non-Conformists by organizing through Barbara Ward "The Sword of the Spirit," and his disarming Yorkshire accent so often heard over BBC tended to dispel the old impression that Catholics were all foreigners. Churchill was much taken by him. Brendan Bracken (a sometime Irish Catholic who had lost both handicaps in an English Public School) usually handled the appointments to Episcopal Sees for the Prime Minister and told his American guest that when there was a vacancy in Canterbury after the retirement of Archbishop Cosmo Gordon Lang, Mr. Churchill who was pacing up and down his office discussing the various candidates, suddenly stopped and asked with a twinkle in his eye, "You don't think we could sell it to Hinsley, do you?" Such, however, was the power of tradition that when the Cardinal died in March the Prime Minister was too busy to attend the funeral and of course the Royal Family could not be even represented. Buckingham Palace had yet to learn that the

Catholic Hierarchy had been re-established some hundred years before; as for Archbishop Godfrey, the first Apostolic Delegate to be appointed since the spacious days of the Great Elizabeth, he would just have to live out his life somehow without ever being invited to a garden party.

While some of these British habits of mind seemed quite immutable, others were visibly changing and as the visitor from New York tramped the London streets and toured the shires, he thought he could catch a glimpse here and there of the future. It was a time of transition. During March there were intermittent air raids, usually about 2 o'clock in the morning. The allies had just sent 1,000 planes over Berlin and Hitler had vowed to reciprocate, so every night people went to bed wondering if this one was to be the "1,000 plane raid." As it happened, the big raid never materialized. No one knew of the buzz bomb that the Germans were preparing, so the gas masks disappeared in April and on May 2nd all the church bells rang for the first time in three years. The war was far from over, but it was felt that the immediate threat to England was past. Our American Jesuit happened to be in Wimpole Street at the moment calling on the shade of Elizabeth Barrett Browning and still remembers the laughter on the sidewalks and the spectacle of Englishmen speaking to perfect strangers. So there would be an end to the blackout, after all, and to barrage balloons and rationing and shabby clothes and houses thirsty for paint—but he wondered would the liberal arts return?

He had read *Humanisme Intégral* and recalled that for Jacques Maritain the problem of humanism had already passed from the professors to the statesmen; that pagan humanism was the two-faced inspiration of the friendly Soviet as well as the hostile Nazis; that the thinkers around "good old Uncle Joe," our "democratic ally," had emancipated the Russian masses from "the illusion called God" and then from the tyranny of private property, leaving the State free to emancipate itself from the "illusion of the human person." How far had this blight spread in the free world? Would Christian humanism ever catch up?

In his midweek travels the Lenten preacher had been a guest at Oxford's Campion House, had dined with the Fellows of Oriel and New College, walking home in the dark through silent streets with the familiar domes and towers silhouetted against the moonlight; had gone to tea and lunch in studies and gardens and a little upstairs restaurant where the sausage was stuffed with a somewhat lower percentage of potatoes; had discussed the future of the liberal arts with Sir David Ross, Sir Gilbert Murray (who had gone to the trouble of looking up everything he could find about Fordham before coming to the party), and Christopher Dawson and Father Martin d'Arcy. They all looked forward to lean years and final uncertainty. The Headmaster of Winchester, very affable in a blue suit and a Roman collar, and Lord Quickswood, the Provost of Eton, a much older man, hoped with some confidence that the classical curriculum had a future. In Cambridge he dined in Hall at the head table for a change, and sipped port afterwards in the Combination Room, and looked up old tutors and Masters of the '20s who might be still around. One was in, but dry and cold, one had gone off boy-scouting, two were in politics, one was in the army, one had deserted to Harvard, one was senile and one was dead. Everything seemed different. The courts were empty, the streets were crowded and uniforms, all kinds of uniforms, were everywhere. Just to recapture something of the past, the wistful visitor borrowed a bicycle from one of the students at St. Edmund's and rode over to Trumpington and Grantchester. Sure enough, even there he found change. Someone had fixed Rupert Brooke's old clock in the village church tower and the time was correct.

The river was almost deserted. In Birmingham, Archbishop Williams took him out to the Oratory at Edgebaston where he was shocked to learn that with thousands of Americans pouring through the city and and hundreds of thousands of natives living there, no one had been to visit the rooms of John Henry Newman in nearly two months. The Rector could not remember when anyone had said a prayer at his grave. The next morning ghosts were everywhere when a very humble pilgrim mounted the pulpit of the chapel at Oscott to speak to the seminarians. Newman had stood there 91 years before when he preached the Second Spring. Newman? Who was he? And what was the Second Spring?

Back in New York and glad to be there, just as much an American and a Catholic as ever, he probably would have startled his Irish forebears by echoing the words of Alice Duer Miller: "But in a world where England is finished and dead, I do not wish to live."

New York was having what is called a black-out. Compared with London its streets looked normally bright, but Fordham knew that a war was on. 7,850 of its alumni and students were called to the colors before the end, 60 of them as Chaplains. Eventually 225 would make the supreme sacrifice and possibly

2,000 be awarded the Purple Heart. Meanwhile, in common with other colleges and universities throughout the country, Fordham was preparing to cooperate with the Armed Forces. Two units of the Army Specialized Training Program were established on the campus with a maximum registration of 788. The civilian college was reduced to one third of its normal size, the great majority in science. No more Greek plays; the air was full of modern languages, Russian and Japanese, with overtones of basic engineering.

One ray of sunshine struggled through. All the downtown schools were moved out of the Woolworth building. Social Service got a fine location near Grand Central, and the others an even better transportation center at City Hall. Both transactions were in a buyer's market, involved no debt, and sharply reduced the maintenance costs. Neither was much of a help, however, to the struggling liberal arts.

VII

In a Cold War

LIFE IN ENGLAND had been uncertain, but the English were used to it. Back in New York chaos was a novelty. The future was being decided far away and while no one seriously believed that the Axis could win, the destruction might go on until there was nothing left. Higher education was moving into a class with charcoal steaks—something to remember. Deficits were piling up at colleges and universities, except where the efficient Navy had moved in and was sustaining even the football schedule. Institutions which had to depend on the unpredictable Army could hardly plan a year in advance. In the spring

[169]

of 1944, on a week's notice, all the boys in the S.A.T.P. at Fordham were shipped overseas and all too soon found themselves in the Battle of the Bulge, where 22 of them were killed. Meanwhile the civilian registration sank to a new low; 63 in Pharmacy instead of 400, 36 in Business Administration instead of 750; and the Liberal Arts? Seventeen-year-olds and "4Fs."

Suppose the war lasted another five years (and judging from Salerno and Anzio and the South Pacific it might!), would we have the high idealism displayed by the Chinese in the epic flight of their universities? At a time when the lamp of learning was being extinguished all over Europe, when many Americans were willing to see our colleges and universities closed for the duration of the war, thousands of Chinese students and professors migrated hundreds of miles into the interior, carrying their books and instruments on their backs. The distances were great—in some cases it was as though Fordham had moved to Kansas City—and the hardships were incredible, but classes were held even on the road. What is still more remarkable, neither Army nor Government treated these scholars as delinquent in their patriotic duty. It was recognized that China's future greatness was bound up with the greatness of her universities, and that the men who kept the spirit of study alive were serving their country as truly as the soldiers in the field.

Of course this devotion to learning was not a novelty in China. For nearly 4,000 years, advancement in its public life was dependent on passing an intricate series of examinations in a species of the liberal arts. Miles of ancient examination halls in Chengtu and Nanking bear witness to the tradition that made aspiring magistrates and tax collectors master the *Four Books* and the *Five Classics,* made them chant the beautiful odes of Li Tai-po or Tu-Fu and quote the five Philosophers of the Sung dynasty. And some reactionaries wonder if the intellectual atmosphere of our House of Representatives in Washington would deteriorate notably if its members were able to quote Horace and Anacreon and to apply a little of Aristotle's logic.

It is true, of course, that China's ancient ideal of learning presupposed a condition of isolationism which could not endure in the modern world. By 1944 there were no Forbidden Cities or Hermit Kingdoms left. There was very little national privacy of any kind anywhere. Time and space had vanished. Fences were down and for better or worse all the peoples of the world found themselves in one huge sprawling marketplace. But the tradition of reverence for learning was still a vital force in China.

Too many of our own people at the time were willing in the face of an uncertain future to forget all arts but the art of war. It was only the older faculty members still on campus who whispered in corners about getting ready for "a brave new world." They were stubbornly convinced that the liberal arts, which had always spelt human freedom in the past, were more essential than ever and feared what scientism run wild could do to the next generation.

A group of this sort, called Education for Freedom Inc., was formed about this time around an Episcopal rector in Scarsdale, the Rev. James Harry Price, and sponsored a radio program featuring Robert Hutchins, Walter Lippman, Stringfellow Barr, John Erskine, Mortimer Adler and several others. The president of Fordham was glad to join them because he was convinced that our freedom on the home front was at stake in 1944, much as it was in 1776, and that our whole post-war development depended on our freedom.

The present attack of course, was not exactly the same as we had seen in the 18th century. It was more complicated now. Before the Revolution we were faced by George III, a dull, stubborn, frequently mad

ruler who had his own German version of the Stuarts'
Divine Right of Kings. Surrounding him was the cor-
rupt, peculiarly brutalized aristocracy of 18th century
England with its conviction that the Colonials were
children at best, whose principal virtue should be
docility. Theirs was of course one kind of effort to
convince Americans that they had no right to be free.
It was the chief misfortune of his unfortunate reign
that by 1765 the liberal arts were beginning to work
on the American mind. Largely as a result of that
fact, an extraordinary group of leaders arose who
would have done credit to any modern European
country with ten times the population of the Colonies.
They were men who knew their literature, their history, their philosophy. And philosophy for them was
threefold: metaphysical, covering the ground we
speak of as philosophy today (their logic was particularly strong); physical, including most of the scientific knowledge of the time; and moral philosophy,
or ethics. The last, of course, included the rights and
duties not only of a creature but of a citizen as well.
So that when the Declaration of Independence was
written it was not the miraculous inspiration of a
single man or of the group of men with whom he
worked. The penmanship was Thomas Jefferson's,
the juxtaposition of ideas came from the entire group,

but the ideas themselves were taken from a treasure-house that had been filled with pure gold by ancient and medieval thinkers and drawn on for centuries by the literature, history and philosophy of Europe. The farmers of Lexington may not have known Aristotle and Cicero any more than they knew John Locke, but they took their signals from the men who did.

Now, in 1944, it seemed to many that freedom was being threatened again not only in Europe where despair had strengthened the Absolute State and weakened the liberal arts, but here in these same United States of ours. We were face to face with many forms of contemporary propaganda, all striving to convince us in various ways that man is not free, all preparing, consciously or unconsciously, for the Absolute State. Some had disappeared for a while under the surface. Bundism and Communism had retreated into the body politic and, like a malignant scarlatina, were no longer erupting in an ugly rash. The only reminder we had of them was the persistent movement to federalize everything that touched private life. But the form which concerned us more than any of the rest was the kind of educational philosophy found in many of our schools. American parents might not realize that the sort of education their sons were receiving would have more to do with the future interpretation and amendment of the Constitution than all three branches of our Government put together—but such was the fact.

The easiest way to destroy our freedom completely was to cut off one by one the roots that nourished it. This many American educators were doing systematically like their European mentors and the steps, though pretty obvious, were very interesting. First, you cut off the idea that man is made for God. Cripple his aspirations. Get him down to earth. Next, you cut off the idea of the natural law and make morality merely the common denominator of what people usually do. Then cut off the idea of inalienable rights. Make all rights depend on other men, that is, on the omnipotent and omniscient State. Make man himself a smart anthropoid, a small and unimportant chunk of society, better still a machine, a bundle of reflexes. It is less likely then that he will develop a sense of responsibility. He will be a better party man, a better follower. Make his intellect a receptive gelatine stripped of all spiritual power. That does away with the liberal arts automatically, because it does away with the old-fashioned notion that a man can train his faculties by general discipline, that one type of study improves his ability to reason, another his appreciation of beauty. Then, when the basis for general

[175]

training has been removed, nothing is left but to expose the gelatine to a large number of facts carefully selected for purposes of propaganda.

Thus, eventually, you can hope to have a generation of robots who will be capable of taking a submarine apart and putting it together again but quite incapable of analyzing their own opinions. They will be modernized, paganized, dehumanized and ready to suffer incredibly for the Absolute State. They could still be saved, perhaps by a transfusion of Christian humanism—a precious plasma taken from the blood bank which our ancestors have stored up for us. But that would mean the return of the liberal arts, and the Absolute State would never tolerate anything so reactionary. For dictators, whether of the Left or Right, realize quite clearly that when their subjects feel in their veins the quickened pulse of literature, history and philosophy, their brains cells begin to function independently, their shrivelled souls begin to expand, they begin to realize what a creature is man. They even begin to think of God.

Here in the America of 1944 we had not plumbed the depths like half the people of Europe and Asia, but it seemed to Education for Freedom, Inc. that three generations of experiment in education had left their mark on all too many of our fellow citizens.

Too many graduates of high school and college not only could not read or write, but had no idea what life was all about. They did not know why they were here, what they were, and where they came from. They did not know the nature of law or liberty, so that some were all ready to have the most precious thing in the world taken away from them in exchange for lower taxes, or a cheaper automobile, or an automatic dishwasher. Surprisingly enough the program struck sparks at once. The radio audience sent in an average of 1,000 letters a broadcast, many critical. There were pointed articles in *The New Republic, P. M., Current History,* and *Ethical Culture* which accused the speakers of intolerance and branded the liberal arts as a weapon of Fascism. The real difficulty seemed to be the indicated relationship of the liberal arts to the Christian concept of education.

The Humanist devoted the leading article of its spring number to a salty attack by Sidney Hook. This magazine was the mouthpiece of The American Humanist Association which sought "to stimulate development of the naturalistic emphasis in religion, philosophy and life . . . in opposition to all defeatist, escapist or other-worldly viewpoints." What seemed to annoy Mr. Hook particularly was Dr. Adler's remark: "Above all, education for freedom must be dissociated from that false liberalism which makes a travesty of liberal education." "What Adler is actually saying," he snapped, "is that no one can have a reasonable belief and freedom, no one can impart a liberal education who doesn't accept the Aristotelian, Thomistic metaphysics and theology which essentially require an infallible church to interpret the undefined terms of its dogmas and power to enforce its interpretations." After cooling off, Mr. Hook would probably have edited that himself a little, but it did point up the sharp difference between the Christian humanism that some educators were still struggling to preserve, and the sort of pagan humanism that was sure to survive in a mechanistic postwar world.

Meanwhile the international sky showed signs of clearing. Of particular interest to starving educators at the time was passage of the GI Bill of Rights, with its generous scholarships for returning veterans. It sounded a note high in the mountains that better days were ahead.

By the New Year of 1945, events were galloping. A dying Roosevelt started for the Black Sea area to attend a fatal conference. Two months more and he was dead, but his dream-child, the United Nations, convened for the first time in San Francisco with a

Constitution that had the Yalta formula buried in its heart. Germany's surrender was unconditional, Harry Hopkins went to Moscow to tie up a few loose threads, and nothing was left but Potsdam and Hiroshima, so by September 2nd it was all over. We had won the war the hard way. As far as could be seen, we had not missed a single mistake and proceeded, from there on, to lose the peace systematically.

The first step was taken by the folks back home who pressured the Government into premature disarmament. This ultimately disastrous move was an immediate blessing for higher education. It meant first, drops of rain after a drought, then a downpour, then floods. Four thousand eight hundred new registrations at Fordham in a single year! All sorts of rumors had gone the rounds about the psychiatric effects of the war, and it was feared that the veterans would be unsettled, distracted and difficult to direct; that in consequence they would lower scholastic standards. The opposite proved to be the case. They lowered the demand for Latin and Greek but quickly took the lead in maturity and application. It is true that their enthusiasm for college life and student activities had dimmed since high school days. A football rally was a little pale for one who had faced sheets of fire on a beachhead, but scholarship they had dreamed about on sentry duty. In only one thing they disappointed us. We had hoped that after being dominated by machines for four years, they would be hungry for the liberal arts, but in most cases where they sought them out it was with ulterior motives. They were in a highly practical frame of mind, anxious to "get going."

In their absence at various fronts, a School of Adult Education had been organized and, through it, all the resources of the university thrown open to qualified students of every age. It proved invaluable for sincere and determined veterans who were on the mature side and kept the liberal arts alive for hundreds of them.

For those who looked for a modern profession demanding culture, talent, energy and a dash of the apostolic, a new department was formed: the Department of Communication Arts. This offered not only to the students, but to the university as a whole, a tremendous opportunity for public service. After all, the vast majority of our fellow Americans were dependent for their thinking on four sources of information: the press, the radio, the movies, and the stage. TV was still in its infancy. To raise the tone of this gigantic four-fold University of the People by training a professional "faculty" through the liberal arts, was the purpose of this new department which could easily grow into a school. Many hoped that it would. The cooperation of the New York press was easily secured. Editors signed up to teach professional courses in journalism and laboratories were established in the offices of the leading papers. For Drama there were already three campus theatres, the large one with the triple stage, the little theatre in the Graduate School, and the arena theatre for plays "in the round." So that it only remained to open a fully equipped radio station. (The movies could wait for a year.) Station WFUV-FM began in 1946 programming 15 hours a day, with an effective range of 40 miles. It was never intended as a machine shop, but from the beginning was as much an instrument of the liberal arts as the theatre or debate hall. So together with daily Mass for "shut-ins" and the inevitable news summaries, weather reports and sportscasts, there have been so far 14 years of good music and theatre, book reviews, round tables and "Air College" lectures and courses. There were old-timers who called this artificial respiration for the humanities, but it did help a tradition to live a little longer.

Meanwhile some saw light dawning with the educational reforms that began to appear in high places. The ferment of neo-humanism in the early '30s and all the picturesque shouting across Lake Michigan had passed without too much comment from Cambridge and New Haven, but had registered none the less. It took the war which suddenly blew on our necks the hot breath of the Absolute State to make freedom overnight the principal subject of everyone's speculation. The best educators in the country saw at once the connection between freedom and the arts that free—that free men's minds so that they can think straight; so that they can know how they came to be free, and how they should use their freedom. There were stirrings in the ivy on the walls. Chicago, Harvard, Princeton and Columbia in a series of admirable studies reexamined their educational ideals and arrived at conclusions that would have been strangely familiar to the father of the *Ratio Studiorum*. A little later Chicago was able to welcome Yale to the ranks of the reawakened with a slight sniff from the College Dean who wrote that "it's good to have such distinguished company after all these years."

Yale appointed its faculty committee for curriculum reform in 1940 and Harvard in 1943, but the reports were published almost simultaneously in 1945. This was three years after the University of Chicago had voted to award the bachelor's degree at the end of Sophomore, "when the student's liberal educa-

tion had come to an end." The news reports stressed
the word "general" rather than "liberal" but the terms
seemed interchangeable. Both programs limited the
elective principle drastically and emphasized the importance of what we had always called the wisdom
studies, in order to give the students a broad view of
the world with the means of understanding it. The
basic requirements at Yale were English, systematic
thinking (could that be good old logic by any
chance?), and modern languages. Latin and Greek
were done for apparently, and many details and re-
finements were wrapped up in the sacred dialect dear
to educators at conventions, but prospects were
bright for the return of the liberal arts. President Sey-
mour of Yale even recommended that the role of religion in higher education be re-evaluated (it seemed
to be in a class with the Confederate dollar) in order
to offset the prevalent aimlessness and lack of purpose
and to develop students as responsible bearers of
spiritual values.

Harvard felt that "religion is not now for most colleges a practicable source of intellectual unity," so it
substituted for religion "belief in the worth and meaning of the human spirit however one may understand
it." Unfortunately there happen to be many various

[183]

ways of understanding the human spirit, and some of them are full of despair.

One such was outlined about this time in the inaugural address of Julian Huxley as Director General of the United Nations Educational Scientific and Cultural Organization. Speaking on the subject, *Unesco: Its Philosophy and Purpose,* he said: "Individuals are meaningless except in relation to the Community . . . In the ultimate interests of mankind as a whole the spread of man must take second place to the conservation of other species . . . Progress is the raising of the upper level of the 'world stuff' of which we as well as the stars are made." This conforms to "a scientific world humanism" which will not tolerate "religious prejudice or cultural obscurantism." One could almost hear Heine's enlightened sneer: "On your knees! Do you not hear the tinkling of the bell? The Last Sacraments are being brought to a dying God."

VIII

In a Crystal Ball

It was in this uncertain atmosphere of exploration that Fordham decided to have another Centenary celebration. The effects of the Centenary of Foundation had been wiped out by Pearl Harbor and the four unpredictable years that followed, but fortunately there was still the Centenary of the Charter to fall back on.

The President of the United States, Harry S. Truman, was honored with a degree at a ceremony held on the Terrace of the Presidents, so called because five other Heads of State had been received there. Mr. Truman's address was a great success, and should have prepared his hearers better than it did for his un-expected second term. But on reflection, many years after, it is interesting to note that throughout the observance of the Charter Centenary, in spite of the generous participation of the Board of Regents and the State Department of Education, the liberal arts were practically ignored. With the exception of a lecture or two on history that was mostly political philosophy, the discussions and speeches were in such fields as modern education, juvenile delinquency, and chemo-therapy. No one at the Convocation or the Dinner even quoted the old standby, *Moribus antiquis res stat Romana virisque.*

Perhaps it was that by 1946 too many new consolations and discouragements were crowding in from every quarter.

The new prosperity was an especially welcome distraction. Although the days of lavish federal loans were still to come, it was possible now to get on with a new residence for graduate students, a campus branch for the School of Business, enlargement of the library facilities and, best of all, a suitable War Memorial for the 229 wonderful boys we had lost. Consolation came also with the increased support given for research. From a modest beginning in 1939 when three foundations gave a total of $3,650 for projects in political philosophy, labor law and physics, the grants for such purposes steadily increased so that from 1942–1948 there was a total of nearly a quarter of a million dollars from 21 sources, in addition to another quarter of a million for radio and student aid.

Even this seems very modest now that immense national wealth and smart tax lawyers have raised an incredible crop of foundations. In 1940 there were only 400 of them in the whole country. In 20 years the number has increased until it reaches 5,000 big ones and 7,000 little ones, with family foundations burgeoning at the rate of 100 a month.

More significant than the mere increase of foundations was the interest in the liberal arts that began to appear in the business world. Pessimists had about decided that if we were to meet our obligations in the matter of faculty salaries, the colleges would have to beg the money from the Federal Government, a prospect that made private institutions fear for their independence.

Then suddenly, almost without warning, the sky began to brighten. The colleges saw a new way out of this dark dilemma. It was no longer to be "hell or Connaught," extinction or Federal Aid. There was now a *tertium quid* in sight—Big Business. This time, however, it was not the liberal arts that had changed, but the men in the marketplace. Great corporations, schooled in world trends, and now thoroughly frightened by what they had seen, began to extend the word "useful" until it covered not only the things of the counting-room but even the things of the spirit. As a result, an increasing number of gifts were announced, some like Henry Ford's two hundred and fifty million dollars for teachers' salaries, that are aimed exclusively at the preservation of the liberal arts, while others like the Sears-Roebuck and Time-Life benefactions, by making scholarships available in any college of the winner's choice, are aimed in the vast majority of cases at benefiting the cause. Similar appropriations are now confidently expected from enlightened labor unions as well as from the stockholders of oil and automobiles, for all responsible businessmen in the ranks of labor and management seem more than ever to have something in common. They seem to be going conservative in the best sense of that much abused word.

There was a time when big business was too often identified with wild speculation and the unions with disorder. It was so in the days of the Fisks and Goulds and Vanderbilts and even later when Morgan and Hill and Harriman held the spotlight while the country held its breath. They rocked the United States

Treasury with their battles for the Erie Railroad and the Knickerbocker Trust, but today big men are fighting for very much higher stakes without rocking anything in Washington. Responsible labor leaders and financiers are beginning to fight for the preservation of our way of life. And this they are doing not only because they are in private life fathers of families, citizens of their country and creatures of Almighty God who can see in a worldwide threat to our Western inheritance, a threat to their homes, their country and their religion, but because as businessmen guided by the profit motive, they need our way of life; they need peace and freedom and integrity and above all, perhaps, hope. Despair, the spirit of modern culture, is bad for business as it is for everything else.

Meanwhile the registration at Fordham, more of a distraction than a consolation, was building up to an all time high of 13,200, a dizzy increase of 10,000 in six years. The treasurer's office was enchanted, of course, but those responsible for the official policy of selectivity had reason for anxiety. Only constant pressure from the Governor and the State Department of Education always to take "just 200 more"; only their generosity in providing nine temporary buildings to be removed in five years when the university could return to reasonable proportions, broke down the re- sistance of the head office.

It was about this time that the President of the University served on an Advisory Committee for a survey that Elmo Roper was doing for *Fortune*. The object was to determine just what the American peo- ple look for in higher education. As *Fortune* summed up the results, "It would seem that relativism had gone rampant, yet the layman, not to say the educa- tor, could do worse than ask himself whether or not there is such a thing as truth about education, or for that matter about anything else. If there is, the safe conclusion from this survey, is that neither the Amer- ican people nor on the whole, their educators have found it."

From the tabulation of the figures, it would seem that the benefactions of Big Business had begun too late. While 62% of our fellow citizens wanted their boys in college, only 3% were interested in their fitness to be there. 66% considered job preparation the pri- mary object, and 2% culture. Only 31% would allow even half the time in college to be spent on the liberal arts. But when asked if it were true that a large num- ber of young people were in college who did not be- long there, 53% agreed that it was so.

Thus even the man-in-the-street could see the rapid

expansion downward of American Education. The era of mass production was well under way. During the period between 1900 and Pearl Harbor, the population of the country doubled but the high-school population was multiplied ten times, from half a million to five million. So too in higher education. In 1900, 4% of the college-age group was in college. At the outbreak of the war, 14%; at the close of the war, 22%. But this increase unfortunately reflected an increase of prosperity and the desire for business and social advantage, rather than an increase in intellectual capacity, or even intellectual curiosity.

Clearly then, a government study was in order to discover some way of directing this expensive and limited thing called higher education into the channels where it would do the most good to the country. We needed some just and scientific process of eliminating on a grand scale unqualified teachers and students. So President Truman wisely appointed a distinguished committee on higher education to advise him. Early in 1948 they issued their unfortunate report.

It was unfortunate because in it terms or slogans were used which, properly defined, everyone must support, but which were associated with realities which everyone must condemn. The terms them-

[193]

selves, "the democratic spirit in education" and "equality of opportunity," are admirable and redolent of the 18th century. They would have aroused as much enthusiasm in Thomas Jefferson and Benjamin Franklin as "life, liberty, and the pursuit of happiness," but the Founding Fathers could not have understood the mass education of today any more than they could our mass production in Detroit; still less could they have grasped the modern failure to distinguish between the process of making a machine and the process of making a man. What the Commission on Higher Education was really calling for was educational inflation, educational fraud. They wanted to spread our national culture perilously thin and call it "democracy of education." They wanted to swell the number of incompetents in American colleges and call it "equality of opportunity."

Small effort was made to enumerate or analyze our present startling failures at the high school and college level, failures which would be multiplied and intensified if all the recommendations of the Commission had been carried out. Instead, they offered a panacea for the intellectual and moral crisis through which the country was passing at the time. Their panacea was more and more advanced schooling, even if it be—as it must be—inferior. Briefly they wanted, by

[194]

1960, 4,600,000 students in higher education in place of the 1,500,000 that were normal before the war, and the 2,254,000 that were forced on us at the close of the war with a peak load of 1,000,000 veterans. They called for a faculty of 350,000 persons, although we could not possibly have in so short a time half that number qualified to teach at the university level. Real teachers cannot be turned out on the assembly line. How many presidents have thought to themselves when signing diplomas in June, "Doctors are made by fools like me but only God——" and then the rhyme stopped them.

It is true that on the basis of the World War II Army General Classification Test, the experts expected to have 4,600,000 ready for higher education in 1960. But I know no educator with reasonably high ideals would admit that we have half that number ready today. The effects of such misplaced optimism are only too obvious. Its defenders try to tell us that college standards are not diluted when the masses pour in—at least not necessarily. That's what they said about Lend Lease: it would not necessarily lead to war. That's what they said about Prohibition: it would not necessarily dull the conscience of the people. That is what wild speculators have always said about unsecured currency, that it would not necessarily lead to financial ruin. But in all these cases we have always dealt with the loftiest probabilities. When the masses poured into the high schools forty years ago, the old high schools did not bring the masses up to their level. The masses brought the high schools down to theirs. At the close of the Second World War, our colleges and universities had just a taste of what will be in store for them if educational inflation is unchecked. By 1948 they found themselves understaffed and overcrowded, conducting a program which was sneeringly called "a silent conspiracy to defraud the public and the Government." That, of course, was an unfair criticism since the terrific pressure to take more students than the better colleges wanted had come to them from the Government and the public. It was patriotism at that time to do what they could in a situation that was regarded as a temporary phase, but they realized that the promoting of anything like 4,600,000 products of American high schools into higher education would suffocate with mediocrity any college or university that got on the bandwagon of inflation.

It is always necessary then to be on our guard against those dangerous slogans, "democracy of education" and "equality of opportunity." It has been a normal condition of American colleges for years that one-third of the so-called students were in the way, cluttering up the place and interfering with other people's intellectual progress. If more room is needed to take care of the expected population boom from postwar babies, it can be created in good part by clearing out the useless lumber that is already on the campuses. That would be like adding one new institution to every two in existence.

If only we could confine our efforts to the educable, we might find enough good teachers to educate them. But the proper screening of students is a principle which the American people find difficult to accept. It is not supposed to be democratic. The public still regards advanced study as a kind of tribal initiation with no intellectual implications.

Thus the President's Commission emphasized the staggering increase that could be expected soon in young Americans of college age, but held out little hope that they would be better prepared for college in 1960 than they were in 1948. It urged however the building of more and more bigger and bigger institutions so that the unqualified might not be discriminated against. This meant enormously increased facilities for getting a college degree and sharply decreased facilities for getting a college education.

Ignoring the rare opportunity that the postwar

pressure presented of squeezing out the watered stock and improving our national standards, the Commission seemed determined that our sprawling educational pattern would continue to sprawl so that no one in our democracy would ever have the humiliation of knowing less than anyone else. The next Commission on Higher Education should certainly include at least a sprinkling of jaundiced and disillusioned ex-college presidents.

So now half a century has passed over our heads since a freshman at Georgetown first became conscious that the poor old liberal arts were in strategic retreat. It has been no ordinary struggle all these years. It has been a struggle with Principalities and Powers; some of them out in the open, some of them invisible strategists alert and much too clever, some of them disembodied philosophies and some just blind unreasoning forces. At no point in the fifty years has there been a frontal attack. No one of importance has said: "Away with culture. Technology is enough for us. Away with wisdom. We want only facts." The enemy has followed rather the military tactics made famous by the Macedonian cavalry. Like fleet horsemen they have relied on an enveloping movement, while the ancient phalanx of the liberal arts has been steadily giving ground all these years, fighting a rear-guard action, the hardest of all battles to win.

Fifty years ago the old ideal which Newman saw as the aim of a liberal education—"nothing more or less than intellectual excellence," to be achieved by a process of training in which the intellect "is disciplined for its own sake, for the perception of its own proper object and for its own highest culture" —still seemed desirable and attainable, though we knew that challenge was in the air. We still identified the "highest culture" with Christian humanism, and our favorite way of becoming Christian humanists involved a first-hand knowledge of Greek and Roman classics.

Our persistence in defending our favorite way was not vestigial; it was not a mere habit that was formed in a simpler time when men had less to learn and much more leisure. It was a matter of dispassionate conviction arising from arguments that seem as valid now as they were in 1909. Now as then it is desirable to know some other civilization with familiarity, in order that we may better know our own. Now as then the splendor, depth and completeness of Greece and Rome are more impressive than that of Russia,

Carthage or Victorian England, not to mention Rooseveltian America or the worm-eaten and distracted Europe of the 20th century. They will always have moreover immensely greater value than any other civilization as being two of the principal fountainheads of modern life.

Now, as then, a fully sympathetic understanding of another civilization involves a knowledge of its language. When the further advantage is added that these particular languages are themselves so beautifully and so logically developed that their mastery tends to form invaluable habits of the intellect, it is clear why their present neglect is regarded in some circles with such anxiety. It is true that where the spirit of Christian humanism is intact, and the teacher is himself a trained classicist, his students can derive real benefit from good translations, Yet the humanist spirit is fading, and trained classicists are disappearing, so that extracts from the *Odyssey* are becoming embalmed paragraphs in another dead survey-course —than which nothing can be more deadly!

We never held that the approach through the literature of Greece and Rome was the only way to reach the culture we always associated with the liberal arts. In Cambridge we had an example to prove that any one of the wisdom studies will do, if the purpose and spirit of the faculty and student body are genuinely humanistic. But in most American colleges, faculty and students alike are losing interest in the old objectives. They say they are humanists who have abandoned naturalism, when all they have given up is the name. As a philosophy for modern times, any sort of naturalism should have lost its charm by now. It should have been recognized as a failure because it always shuts its eyes to reality. It gives man a picture of nature which man discovers to be false as soon as he tries to live by it. Those who cling to it, through prejudice against the spiritual or the supernatural, never find harmony, order or inner peace. For either they come to regard themselves as a part of nature, one phenomenon in the midst of a million others, "a thing of ghastly irrelevance," or realizing that they are not one with nature, they can have no principle of order since they have given up God.

What has immunized so many educators from the effects of logic in this matter has been most of all a world war which began nearly a half a century ago. Hot, cold, or indifferent, it has never let up its strident emphasis on the physical and mechanical aspects of nature. This has indirectly strengthened the appeal of relativity, with its fuzzy thinking on absolute truth;

psychologism, with its ambition to dissect human nature as one would the brain cells of a frog; scorn of tradition, which has nothing to learn from the past; methodicism, with its worship of "how" at the expense of "what"; scepticism, which concentrates on the pursuit of truth rather than truth itself; and scientism, which accepts the laboratory as the only source of truth. But regardless of the degree to which any of these may be responsible for the situation, it is more true than ever that science is now the main instrument of our national education; that by its predominance it is still dehumanizing our schools; that it is more than ever crowding out our liberal arts, and that all the grand plans for reforming the curriculum and strengthening humanism which roused such hopes in the forties, have been powerless to counteract its influence.

It would be consoling to report that the Jesuit Colleges are unaffected by the national trend and that the *Ratio Studiorum* is holding its own, but such is not the case. Our ideals and purposes are in general just what they were 400 years ago. We shall never be tempted to intellectual suicide by adopting naturalism under any alias, and no philosophy of education could ever interest us which is found to be a blend of socialism, pragmatism and exaggerated experimentalism. We esteem the individual too highly to be thorough-going socialists. We are too devoted to principles which we regard as eternal to be entirely pragmatic. We are too impressed by the accumulated wisdom of the human race, by that treasure of experience to which each generation adds its small deposit of gold, ever to have our schools ignore the past and start again as though no one else had ever lived before us.

But that does not mean that we are unaffected by the national trends. We are conducting American colleges and do not dare to be too different. Our students come to us conditioned by the postwar atmosphere they breathe, the only one they have ever known. For most of them that atmosphere creates a close association between a degree and a future salary. It is a far cry from the days when university graduates were expected to be teachers, statesmen, gentlemen of leisure, or clerics. The value of the classical tradition for such was always fairly obvious. Today it has to be sold to a resisting public. As for the colleges themselves, the financial and administrative problems are not what they used to be. It was one thing to receive a foundation of so many golden ducats from the Duke of Gandia or the Municipality of Hildesheim so that one could operate in tranquility as a free school, and quite another to begin in a log cabin or an office building and live on tuition. Even 50 years ago the presidents of our older institutions were dignified and scholarly men in immediate contact with their handful of pre-war students. Now we have to find the type that can stay out late and wake up cheerful on the alkaline side, eat rich food and keep the figure down, shake hands like a Rotarian, pass the tambourine, and keep the peace among hundreds of faculty members. Under the circumstances we cannot be surprised if our colleges are not too different from their neighbors.

At Fordham for example, as of September 1959, there were 543 Freshmen enrolled in the College of Arts and Sciences. 48% were candidates for the B.S.II, i.e. social science; 27% for the B.S.I, i.e. natural science; 24% for the A.B., with 5% taking college Greek. What of St. Peter's College, which in 1930 issued such a bold declaration of independence? Without comment we give the figures: total Freshmen, 435; B.S.II—business administration as well as social science, 58%; B.S.I—natural science 27%, A.B. 14%, with 2% taking college Greek. Twenty-five years ago the figures for St. Peter's were: A.B. 50%, with 25% taking college Greek.

Obviously the general direction here, as everywhere, is away from the arts towards science—natural science and social science. The Dean's office may explain that a B.S. in Social Science is really an A.B. for non-Latin students, and it may be just that. Where it is, the liberal arts have not vanished with Latin and Greek. But that supposes the strong coordinating power of philosophy and a faculty of thoroughly seasoned humanists. Otherwise it may just be another way of collecting tuition from nice young people who cannot qualify for an A.B. or a B.S.I.

What then can we expect 50 years from now? Any sort of answer will have to depend on shameless crystal-gazing, unless we can be generous with our "ifs." So "if" the human race is still in business and "if" our country is still free, Christian humanists will still be struggling against powerful odds. "If" the Jesuits still have colleges of their own, they will still be talking about the *Ratio Studiorum* and some will be wishing that the old days could return when Horace was in Freshman and Demosthenes in Sophomore. In any case we have reason to hope that their chief purpose will still be the training of the intellect and will; their principal subjects, divine and human nature with the rest of nature as a background; and their principal instruments literature, history, philosophy and theology, with enough pure science to suit their purpose. By then, if they have learned a lesson from the intervening years, only those will be admitted to the liberal arts course who can profit by it. Schools of technology, schools of crafts and trades, professional schools and semi-professional schools will look after the other young people who may be every bit as intelligent but are different from those who ought to be enrolled in the arts. Due to the historic and philosophic and economic influences already mentioned, the shadow of vocationalism, the constant demand for *ad hoc* training comes today from parents and students alike. Their consequent loss of confidence in the value of the traditional arts course would vanish, perhaps, if schools with irreconcilable purposes existed side by side, frankly different, without any effort at compromise; the large and numerous ones teaching the student how to make a living, the small and scattered ones how to live a full, rich, intellectual life. It is true that most of the undergraduates who will thus be able to give their hours to the things of the spirit, will have to learn eventually how to make a living too. For them, however, vocationalism can wait on culture and be taken in stride after graduation, the time element being adjusted by giving the baccalaureate at the end of three shining years.

Aside from wishful thinking, however, the only clue we have to a possible change in the trend away from the liberal arts is the wavelike movement which has so far been a characteristic of human history. Up to the present every trough has been followed by a crest. It was old Lupus, the learned Abbot of Ferrières, who coined a Latin word for it 1100 years ago—*reviridicentia litterarum.* "The growing green again of letters."